THE MIRROR OF CHARITY

THE
MIRROR OF
CHARITY

The *Speculum Caritatis* of
ST. AELRED OF RIEVAULX

Translated and arranged by
GEOFFREY WEBB AND ADRIAN WALKER

WITH AN INTRODUCTION AND NOTES

THE CATHOLIC BOOK CLUB
121 CHARING CROSS ROAD
LONDON, W.C.2

Nihil obstat: ANDREAS MOORE, L.C.L.
Imprimatur: E. MORROGH BERNARD, *Vic. Gen.*
Westmonasterii, die 11a *Decembris,* 1961

First published in 1962

Reproduced by photo-lithography at the Pitman Press, Bath

INTRODUCTION

THERE is an intriguing similarity between the story of Saint Aelred's conversion, and an episode recorded in the *Life of Bernard* concerning a group of young knights who paid a visit to Clairvaux which was destined to change their lives completely. They were hospitably received, and as they rode away from the monastery, the impression that it had made on them increased so overwhelmingly that in next to no time they were back again, 'renouncing their worldly ways and enlisting as soldiers in the fight against Satan'.[1] As William of Saint Thierry insists, when he tells the story, the change in their lives could be considered quite specifically as a diversion of their normal way of life into another channel. From having been soldiers in the world, they dedicated themselves to spiritual warfare against the enemy of God. Being already formed in a noble, military code in which bravery and bounty were as much *de rigueur* as exclusiveness and elegance, they had in effect only switched the battle on to the level of *Psychomachia*,[2] the fight for man's soul. The enemy against whom they now had to take up arms was Sensuality in her jewelled chariot, surrounded by her handmaids, Frivolity, Flirtation, Carnal Love, Beauty and Pleasure. Idolatry must be overcome by Faith, Pride by Humility, Wrath by Patience. It was the crusade against the Saracens fought on the higher plane of the individual's spiritual life. When it was done, the cleansed body and soul would become a holy of holies, a place where Solomon's temple might be built anew, and the heavenly Jerusalem come down and take possession.

At Clairvaux, Bernard often recruited young men of this noble and military stamp, and throughout Europe no doubt it was the same. These were the finest possible raw material for the Cistercian observance. Aelred, in England, was just such a well-found youth, all ready for God in virtue of his training at a noble court, and in his conversion to Cistercian life, we can see in him a most enthusiastic follower of Saint Bernard. The austerities and hard labours of the fight for holiness appealed to him. In his *Mirror of Charity* we can see this in his constant reiteration of the word *labor*, and in his refusal to minimize any single hardship of the monastic life. We see it in his loathing of any sort of decorative element in the monastery buildings, whether of sculpture or painting, or in anything grandiose or unnecessary, right down to 'the glittering of golden vessels and the blaze of candles'. Even the more developed kinds of church music, with the accompaniment of instruments, was anathema to him, since 'the church has outgrown the stage of types and figures', and these things of the senses were only valid in the Old Testament as a hint of the truth that was yet to come. On these matters, Aelred speaks as a true disciple of Bernard, with whom he shares a real passion for all that is denuded, unpolished and unadorned.

Now we must remember that this true Cistercian love for the sober and the moderate, the 'little chapel of rough unpolished stone, where there is nothing carved or painted to distract the eye', is only the necessary complement, and the logical consequence, of an extreme concentration on the monastic aim, which the white monks unanimously placed in charity. Saint Benedict in his Rule called the monastery a 'school of the Lord's service',[3] and from its very beginnings, the Benedictine reform at Cîteaux under Saint Stephen Harding (whose constitutions were called the *Charta Charitatis*) had defined the Lord's service as an exalted ideal of love. Saint Bernard, who did more than anyone else to put the Cistercian reform on the map, emphasized this ideal in all that he did, and all that he wrote. Each Cistercian author added his individual variations to the theme, to the extent that when we speak of the Cistercian school of spirituality, we think not so much of a school of thought as a shared ideal of charity, unfolded in a variety of aspects, through manifold experiences.

Saint Aelred admits that the one great problem of his life was the adjustment of love. He felt, looking back on his youth, that love had made him a pagan. But in the first Cistercian monastery that he visited, he saw at once how love could make him a saint. To do away with the downward-moving lusts of cupidity, to strive after the upward-moving love of charity, all this meant a hard, austere life, but the prize he could see was infinitely more than worth the labour. As a true Christian lover, Aelred is revealed as a complete success in his major works, *Spiritual Friendship* and the *Mirror of Charity*. He achieved a degree of understanding, forbearance and forgiveness which amazes us, and his biographer Walter Daniel can add little to what his works tell us about him, for they might all have been inspired by the words he quotes so lovingly: *Ecce quam bonum* . . . 'Behold how good and how pleasant it is for brethren to dwell together in unity'.

Many people are already familiar with the lovely dialogues of *Spiritual Friendship* in the excellent translation of Dr. Hugh Talbot.[4] The *Mirror of Charity* is a more ambitious work, and one which shows considerable manipulation on the part of the author. Aelred took his time over it, put it aside and forgot it, took it up again only to change his mind about the plan he would follow, adding and intercalating as he went along. Inevitably the book is rather difficult to visualize as a unity, and much patient work must be done before we can know exactly what form the work originally took. But when we examine it, we discover that there is one co-ordinating theme which allows us to see the work in some degree of unity, just as it becomes apparent that some of the additions are by no means essential to the book as a whole. Since our purpose in translating the *Mirror of Charity* has simply been to give the essence of Aelred's teaching on love, we have omitted the disquisitions he added on subjects like free will and minor monastic observances, summarizing them in the appendix at the end, so that the theme of the work might emerge more clearly.

The centre of gravity of the *Mirror of Charity* is in its third section, where we find something which seems to be the original nucleus of the work. There we are given the co-ordinating idea of three Sabbaths of charity—the love of self, of our fellow men, and of God. Like other Cistercians, Aelred saw the true Christian (and *a fortiori* the true monk) as a complete lover: as a soul whose capacity for love must be filled to the brim. It is no accident that in Aelred's imagery, the loving faculty is a container which we must always be endeavouring to enlarge so that everything and everyone lovable may find room in it. He bids his anchoress sister bind all the world into her heart with a bond of love and pity. He speaks of the heart as a hospice, or as a Noah's ark in which all different kinds of men are compared, according to their temperaments, to the birds, beasts and reptiles that survived the flood. There must be room for everyone, for a true lover of God must demonstrate his charity by loving himself in the manner that God wishes, and every member of the human race—whether as friend, relative, stranger or enemy. This is the theme of Aelred's *Mirror*—the search for three loves, of God and self and fellow men, which he sees as the allegorical meaning behind the Sabbath laws of the Old Testament.

The three Sabbaths are seen at their best and completest in the third section, where they are followed by an analysis of love into charity and cupidity. Here Aelred considers the right and wrong uses of love, bringing in the favourite Cistercian image of a love that leads upward, to God, spiritualizing the soul, and of a love which is lust that drags us down to flesh and earth and destruction. In either case it is love, a capacity which our free will can use either for beatitude or damnation, according to whether it is used as God's law decrees, or for the sake of selfish possessiveness. The section finishes with a beautiful little treatise which recalls the thoughts of *Spiritual Friendship*.

The co-ordinating theme of the Sabbaths we find likewise in the first section of Aelred's *Mirror*, which strikes one as being, possibly, an introduction penned at a later date. It may be that Aelred thought to improve on the third section, which already seems complete and perfect enough in our eyes, by introducing the subject with an impressive avenue of theology. In the third section, the Sabbaths have no preamble at all, but the first section begins with an exposition of the creation, which leads up to the appearance on earth of the first man with his special capacity for loving God. The search for happiness, real human happiness, necessarily implies a complete turning away from sin. The whole of human nature needs to be 'circumcised' from sin, and peace of soul can only come with virtue and a clean conscience. Charity is the soul's true Sabbath, and Aelred connects each of the days of creation with one of seven virtues, so that charity may coincide with the day on which God rested from His handiwork. God's rest, for Aelred, is even more wonderful than His creation, since it supplies the moment for reflecting that 'love is His reason for creating, guiding and planning all things from beginning to end'. We can detect the same innocent wonder in these words as in Mother Julian's 'Love is His meaning', or the question of Saint Francis of Sales: 'When did God begin to love you? . . . Never, for He has always been God, without beginning and without end.' Everything in creation is marked with charity. It is the divine imprint in creation, and because man bears that imprint, he must seek for happiness and for rest.

ix

Thus the idea of the Sabbath is as useful for proving, in part I, 'the excellence of charity from its own innate dignity', as it is in part III, where it explains 'how charity is to be manifested and exercised'. The intervening part II is designed to refute some 'stupid objections' to the religious life, and here Aelred goes immediately to the fundamental principles involved. Penance is necessary in the Christian life because of the threefold concupiscence which results from the fall—the lust of the flesh, the lust of the eyes, and the pride of life. From the negative viewpoint at least, these are the things which explain the meaning of the monastic life. Mortification is necessary in the fight against sin and the tendency to sin, and as Aelred explains, if a monk finds his vows a burden, he must not find fault with them, but with his own insufficiently mortified concupiscence. The Cistercian life, if not the hardest to be found in Aelred's time (there were always the Carthusians), was at least far more austere than, for instance, the Benedictine, Augustinian or Premonstratensian observances. Many would have liked to become Cistercians, no doubt, but criticized the way of life as being unrealistically harsh. Aelred makes a particular point of introducing, in this connection, a disputation with an Augustinian canon, who maintained that the keeping of the Rule was not essentially a matter of observing regulations. And he deals more extensively still with those who argue that an austere mode of life necessarily militates against the spiritual consolation which is the acknowledged reward of a life which mortifies the flesh. Such an idea is anathema to Aelred, who draws generously on his own experience to analyse the various kinds of consolation that may occur in the spiritual life. His discussion of this matter is a masterly piece of psychological dissection, which he enlivens by charitably teasing a fervent young novice.

Thus, briefly, one might summarize the work in its three

parts, in order to describe its basic unity, although it is impossible to make any adequate analysis because (even setting aside the obvious digressions) the medieval *speculum* form is not that of a logically argued treatise. As Aelred says in his introductory letter to the abbot of Clairvaux, there are various themes running through it. It tends always to move spiralwise round its subject, carrying along in its course a host of ideas that might seem to be, strictly speaking, irrelevant. The best way to read Aelred in the original is to allow oneself to drift along the movement of his contemplation, and one can at least suggest that the same method might best be followed when reading him in translation. A *speculum* achieves its effect precisely by reflecting its subject matter from many different vantage points, and since it is a more subjective form of writing, the ultimate co-ordinating factor is, of course, the author's own personality. Aelred's genius for friendship is the thing that epitomizes his character, as his biographer and all the commentators on his work observe. God's right to man's love, and the kinship that binds all creation together, are the fundamental intuitions that explain Aelred's concept of charity as *concordia*. As we listen to his words, and visualize him in the great Yorkshire monastery where he effected peace and love among his several hundred monks and brothers, we are struck by the all-embracing optimism of his ideas on friendship. He shares with his master, Saint Bernard, a deep compassion for fallen mankind when his thoughts turn to the weighty matter of the soul's responsibility for sin. But he shares, too, the mentality of William of Saint Thierry, who sought, in his *Meditations*, for the face of God, and found it shining through the faces of the pure in heart.

G. W.
A. W.

CONTENTS

PAGE

INTRODUCTION V

PART I

CHAP.

1. THE CREATOR AND HIS CREATURES 1
2. NATURE, BEAUTY AND PURPOSE ARE PROPER TO ALL CREATURES 3
3. MAN, GOD'S IMAGE, IS MEANT FOR BEATITUDE . . . 4
4. THE IMAGE CORRUPTED BY DISOBEDIENCE AND SELF-LOVE . 5
5. THE IMAGE RENEWED BY OUR SAVIOUR 7
6. THE CORRUPTION OF LOVE 9
7. THE RESTORATION OF THE IMAGE BY LOVE 11
8. CHARITY AND CUPIDITY 12
9. FREE WILL, AND THE CHOICE BETWEEN GOOD AND EVIL . 13
10. CHARITY IS ALL-PERFECT 14
11. CHARITY IS SPIRITUAL CIRCUMCISION 16
12. CHARITY, THE TRUE SABBATH OF THE SOUL . . . 17
13. THE SEVENTH DAY 18
14. GOD'S WORK AND REST 21
15. CHARITY'S MARK IN EVERY CREATURE 22
16. THE DESIRE FOR PERFECT HAPPINESS 23
17. THE DESIRE FOR HEALTH AND RICHES 25
18. SAINTS AND SINNERS AMONG THE RICH 27
19. THE INSTABILITY OF WORLDLY FRIENDSHIPS . . . 28
20. THE PERFECTION AND PRE-EMINENCE OF CHARITY . . 29
21. THE DAYS OF CREATION AND THE VIRTUES . . . 31
22. THE OTHER VIRTUES IN RELATION TO CHARITY . . . 34

PART II

1. RECAPITULATION OF PART I 38
2. THE SOUL'S EFFORT 39
3. PEACE FROM CHARITY 40

CHAP.		PAGE
4.	THE THREEFOLD CONCUPISCENCE	42
5.	THE NECESSITY OF PENANCE	43
6.	TEACHING OF SCRIPTURE ON PENANCE	44
7.	SPIRITUAL CONSOLATIONS	47
8.	COMPUNCTION IN SAINTS AND SINNERS	48
9.	THE PURPOSE OF CONSOLATION	50
10.	GOD'S WORK IN THE SOUL	51
11.	THE FRUITS OF GOD'S VISITATIONS	53
12.	GOD'S CONSOLATION AS THE SOUL'S STRENGTH	54
13.	THE MEASURE OF HOLINESS	56
14.	THE PATH OF PERSEVERANCE	58
15.	CONVERSATION WITH A NOVICE	60
16.	THE WILL AS LOVE	64
17.	THE VARIOUS FRUITS OF COMPUNCTION	66
18.	MORE ADVICE TO A NOVICE	68
19.	ZEAL IN PROGRESSING	70
20.	THE CURBING OF THE FLESH	71
21.	THE PLEASURES OF HEARING	72
22.	THE WANDERING OF THE EYES	74
23.	VANITY	77
24.	THE DESIRE FOR POWER	77

PART III

1.	THE THREE SABBATHS	80
2.	THREE KINDS OF LOVE	81
3.	THE FIRST SABBATH, WHICH IS THE LOVE OF ONESELF	84
4.	THE SABBATH OF BROTHERLY LOVE	85
5.	THE LOVE OF GOD IS A SAFEGUARD FOR ALL OTHER LOVES	88
6.	THE PERFECT SABBATH IN THE LOVE OF GOD	91
7.	LOVE, CHARITY AND CUPIDITY	93
8.	THE RIGHT AND WRONG USES OF LOVE	94
9.	THE CHOICE OF GOOD	96
10.	LOVE MOVES US TO DESIRE AND TO ACTION	98
11.	LOVE AND ATTRACTION	99

CHAP.   PAGE

12. RATIONAL AND IRRATIONAL ATTRACTION   .   .   .   100

13. THE ATTRACTION OF FRIENDSHIP   101

14. THE TIES OF KINDRED   102

15. CARNAL ATTRACTION   103

16. WHAT WE ARE TO THINK OF THESE ATTRACTIONS   .   .   104

17. REASON IMPELS US TO LOVE GOD AND OUR FELLOW MEN   .   104

18. A DISTINCTION BETWEEN TWO LOVES   106

19. TWO MORE COMPARISONS ON THE SAME SUBJECT   .   .   107

20. HOW TO RECOGNIZE THE TRUE LOVE OF GOD   .   .   .   110

21. SOME POINTS CONCERNING THE LOVE OF OUR FELLOW MEN   .   112

22. REASONABLE INCLINATIONS   114

23. FRIENDSHIP, BASED ON MUTUAL GOOD OFFICES   .   .   115

24. THE LOVE OF KINDRED   116

25. PHYSICAL ATTRACTION   119

26. THE ORIGIN AND DEVELOPMENT OF ATTRACTIONS   .   .   119

27. THE PRIORITY OF INCLINATIONS   121

28. ACTION TOWARDS GOD AND OUR FELLOW MEN   .   .   123

29. THREE WAYS OF LIFE   124

30. SATISFACTION FOR SIN   127

31. VOLUNTARY SACRIFICE   128

32. THE DUE PROPORTION TO BE OBSERVED IN THE CONSECRATED
     LIFE   130

33. DUTY TOWARDS SELF, AND DUTY TOWARDS ONE'S FELLOW
     MEN   132

34. THE SPIRITUAL MEANING OF NOAH'S ARK   .   .   .   136

35. THE ENJOYMENT OF FRIENDSHIP   137

36. ENJOYING IN THE LORD   140

     COLOPHON   141

     APPENDIX   143

     NOTES   154

XV

THE MIRROR OF CHARITY

PART I

I

The Creator and His creatures

GOD has spread out His heaven over us like a curtain,[5] and there His stars shine, to give us light in our dark world, where forest beasts roam about, seeking to devour us.[6] Above the heavens are the great waters, from whence the rains come to soften the parched earth, which is the soul of man, and to bring forth fruits of oil and wheat and wine.[7] We would labour in vain without the help of God who gives us our daily bread, but we have only to seek in order to find, and when we have found we have only to taste and see how sweet Thou art, O Lord. My soul, unproductive through its dryness, thirsts for Thy gentle rain, so that there may spring up in it that heavenly bread that feeds the angels. Then it will taste a true delight, and cast aside its yearning for the fleshpots of Egypt, the land where Pharaoh demanded a daily toll of bricks, though he gave no straw for their making.[8] O Good Jesus, let Thy voice sound in my ears so that my heart and mind and my inmost soul may learn to love Thee, and the very depths of my heart cleave to Thee, who art my one delight and joy.

But what is this love which I desire, O my God? Unless I am much misled, it is a wonderful delight in the soul, which is the more sweet for being unsullied by passion, more sincere if it is tender, and a source of joy when it embraces all our fellow men. Love may truly be called the heart's own sense of taste, since it enables us to feel Thy sweetness. Love is the eye by means of which we can see that Thou art good. Love is a capacity for God who transcends all things, and whoever loves God gathers God to himself. The more we love God, the more we possess Him, simply because God *is* love: He is charity.[9] Love is God's rich banquet, that so gratifies those who eat at His table and drink deep, that they forget and lose themselves, only to find themselves in Him. And how shall this be done, unless they love Him?

I beg Thee, Lord, to let but a touch of this delight penetrate my soul, and turn the bread of bitterness to sweetness. Give me the smallest morsel of it as a foretaste of what I yearn for in this mortal life, or rather let my hunger and thirst be that foretaste, for to eat is to hunger still more, and to drink is to thirst still more. Let me eat and drink my fill when all may see the glory and delight that are hidden at the present time, and revealed only to those who love Thee. Meanwhile I shall seek Thee by loving Thee, since to advance in Thy love is certainly to seek Thee, and to love Thee perfectly is to have found Thee. Indeed, justice demands that Thy creatures love Thee, for their capacity to love is a gift that Thou hast given them. The irrational and insensible creation cannot love Thee, for that is beyond its nature. It is not called upon to share man's purpose, which is to be happy, and to love Thee. Instead, the beauty and goodness of creatures, with all their different functions, serve rather to help man to find happiness and love.

GOD's being is above all other modes of being. It cannot be communicated to anyone but God, nor can it undergo any change. It is this same God who has given to every creature its nature, its beauty and its purpose. Thus all created things are good and beautiful, and all have a fixed purpose. All this is God's doing. Everything has its being from the highest and incommunicable being. Everything derives its beauty from the supremely and incommunicably beautiful. The same is true for goodness and wisdom, and all the other qualities that creatures possess. Everything created is by its nature good, and by its form beautiful. It has for its purpose the embellishment of the whole of creation. Hence when God looked at all that He had made, He saw that it was good.[10] A thing is good simply because it is made by God. It is beautiful because, as an individual, it is composed of parts that harmonize with each other. It is ordained to fulfil a certain purpose in so far as it performs, in the plan of the universe, a function in accordance with the mode, the time and the place of its existence.

Thus each thing has a place which fits its mode of existence. For example, the proper place of the angels is heaven, and the irrational creation belongs to the earth, but man, who comes between these two realms of earth and heaven, has a paradise which is both corporeal and spiritual. As regards position and duration likewise, everything has been accounted for in God's beautiful design. The angels were all created at the same time, and they will never cease to be. Men are not all created at the same time, but they none the less have eternal life. Irrational creatures have no common moment of beginning, and they will all come to an end.

I must not fail to mention that each creature is endowed

3

with a mode of existence which is in keeping with its nature. Men who are righteous are destined for the happiness of heaven, while sinners pass their eternity in the torments of hell. Inanimate things and brute animals can experience neither joy nor sorrow. Their mode of existence simply provides them with whatever is best for them. The godly man, as we read in the book of Ecclesiasticus, derives nothing but good from things such as water, fire, iron, milk, bread, honey, grapes, oil, clothing, whereas sinners turn them all to an evil use.[11] For this abuse of things a man may not plead that he shares the common lot of the beasts, and does not understand why he should be raised to a place of honour and domination over them.[12] Such a man is often spoken of as a beast, since he has descended to the level of the animals, and that not only by grovelling among the things of earth. It is hard to measure how great a similarity to the beasts has developed in a soul in which the divine likeness, even if not the divine image, has been effaced. But to return to our subject. . . .

We must realize that evil, although it was not created or activated by God, is made to serve a purpose in His plan. Why, indeed, should not God, who is almighty and infinitely good, allow the existence of an evil which cannot in the slightest way interfere with His eternal designs? His omnipotence and kindness are more clearly shown when He turns evil to good effect, making purposeless things fulfil a function, and granting heaven to the sinner.

3

Man, God's image, is meant for beatitude

FROM the moment of his creation, man was endowed not only with being and goodness—as was also the rest of created nature—nor only with beauty and purpose. He was

4

given a capacity for happiness. Now it is obvious that no creature can have being or beauty or goodness from a source within itself, but derives these things from the supreme Being and Beauty and Goodness. The same is true of happiness, since man's beatitude is derived from the supreme Beatitude in whom the saints in heaven find all their joy. This means that man, who is the image of his Creator, must stay close to God by his love and his life, even if it were only for his own good. The Psalmist says that his only good is to cleave to God,[13] and this is true of every man.

To cleave to God in this way is an activity not of the body but of the soul, for the Author of Creation has endowed the soul with three qualities or powers which enable it to share the eternity and wisdom of God, and to taste His sweetness. These three qualities or powers are memory, knowledge and love, which is the same as will. Of these the memory can share in God's eternity, knowledge can share in His wisdom, and love can taste His sweetness. Man can find God in his own image of the Trinity, for memory has never forgotten its Maker, and knowledge identifies that Maker, while love fastens Him in an embrace which precludes all desire for anything else. It is in this way that a man becomes truly blessed.

4

The image corrupted by disobedience and self-love

MAN reaches his true and unceasing happiness by means of these three powers, but it is in the third, namely love, that the foretaste of blessedness is to be found. Now if we are to be happy we must take delight in something, and there can be no delight where love is not also present. The more we love the highest Good, the more delight we find in It, and hence the greater is our happiness. And although the memory may call many different things into the present, and knowledge may grasp the deepest truths, yet if the will is not attracted by these things, no pleasure will be found in them.

Adam was endowed with free will and helped by God's grace, and he could have delighted always in the thought and knowledge of God by loving Him for ever. In this way he would have been blessed eternally. But he was also capable of concentrating his love on less worthy objects, with the result that by turning from the love of God, his heart grew cold and he was doomed to misery. Just as happiness is to be found in cleaving to God, wretchedness is the result of our turning away from God. Adam was given a special dignity as the first of all men, but he did not understand what the Psalmist realized to be as true of the present as it is of the last day, namely that if we estrange ourselves from God we shall perish, and that all those who are false to Him shall be destroyed.[14] It was Adam's misfortune that he did not grasp that those who are disloyal to God through pride, sink into the depths of folly. Whoever dares to claim the likeness of God as a right, deservedly sinks as low as the beasts he so closely resembles.

By misuse of his free will man no longer directs his love to the unchanging source of all goodness, but trains it instead on some less worthy object, his selfishness having impaired his sight. He loses sight of his true good and wanders towards something that is not truly good, and instead of finding any benefit in it, he discovers only loss. By loving himself in a misdirected way, he loses both himself and God. And this is inevitable, and only right, for if any creature should desire to be like God, in a way that God cannot approve, it is made by that very desire less like God. The image of God in man is ruined, even though it

6

is not completely destroyed. Man still retains the memory which resists his desire to forget God, but his knowledge is now subject to error, and his power of loving turns into lust for the things of the flesh. The mark of the Blessed Trinity still remains in his soul, by virtue of the trinity of his spiritual powers. The soul's very substance bears the imprint of the Triune God, for its powers are a trinity, while its substance is a unity. Hence the Psalmist points out that man passes *as an image* and is *disquieted in vain*,[15] thus showing how the human soul possesses a likeness to the Trinity of its very nature, which has since been branded by sin. Forgetfulness damages the remembrance of God, our knowledge of Him becomes clouded with error, and our love is narrowed down to selfish lust.

5

The image renewed by our Saviour

JESUS CHRIST, however, who is Mediator between God and men, has paid the debt which all human nature owed. He has cancelled the bond which stood against us, with the legal demands that our first enemy, in his pride, claimed from us.[16] He has despoiled those princes and powers of evil to which divine justice delivered us, and He has made peace with the Father for us by His sacrifice on the Cross. He repairs our memory by the teaching of Holy Scripture, our reason by the mysteries of faith, and our love by the daily increase of charity. Thus the image of God within us is perfectly reformed when forgetfulness no longer falsifies memory, when knowledge has no error to confuse it, and love is free of cupidity.

Now perhaps you are wondering where and when the image is restored? The peace, the happiness and calm that

7

it brings are found only in heaven, where forgetfulness has no place, where error cannot deceive minds filled with truth, and lust cannot attack hearts that are filled with divine love. In heaven there is nothing but true and eternal love, an eternity spent in the delight of love and the enjoyment of truth, and the beholding of the eternal, true and most lovable Trinity. There alone is the rest and peace of happiness perfectly possessed. Why then are our souls hurrying hither and thither in their anxiety? Why are they taken up with so many different things? Whatever they seek and wherever they seek it, it can be found in one thing alone. Excellence, knowledge, riches, delight—they are all to be found here, and only here, in their most perfect degree.

Does this world's pit of death and miry clay give true excellence? Can there be perfect knowledge in a life lived under the shadow of death? What real delight can be found in this howling waste and boundless desert?[17] There is no excellence in this world which is not set tottering by fear, no knowledge in a man who does not really know himself, no delight in the things of the flesh that does not finally render a man as carnal as any horse or mule. If your pleasure is to be found in glory or riches, you can take none of your wealth with you when death claims you, nor will your worldly glory have any power in the land of the dead. True excellence is to be found only where ambition can yearn for nothing higher, true knowledge only where nothing escapes its grasp, true delight only where nothing can ever lessen pleasure, true riches only where the possession of them can never be exhausted.

It was a sad day for us when we drew away from Thee, O Lord—so sad that, as our exile drags on and on, we long to know when we may come and stand before Thy face. Would that dove's wings were ours,[18] so that we might fly to Thee, and find in Thee our rest! Meanwhile, O Lord

Jesus, I beg Thee to allow my soul to grow wings in the nest of Thy teaching. May my soul embrace Thee who wast crucified for me, and drink the life-giving draught of Thy most sweet blood. May the thought of Thee and of Thy passion obsess my memory, lest the fog of forgetfulness blot out the thought completely. Until I come before Thy face I will shun all knowledge except that of my crucified Lord, lest the untruth of error upset the sound foundations of faith. May all my love be directed to Thy love, instead of seeking after its own useless desires. I pray, with David, that the very ends of the earth may be mindful of the Lord,[19] and I turn to Him, so that I may not seem to ask these blessings for myself alone. May they be mindful, I pray, because the memory of God has become hidden in the minds of men, even though they have not completely lost it, and it is easier to know something long buried in the mind than something freshly implanted in it. Indeed, there must always be some glimmer of the memory of God in the mind. For a fool to say 'there is no God'[20] implies that there must be at least some understanding in his mind of what the word 'God' means.[21]

6

The corruption of Love

WITH David I must admit that the knowledge of God as He is in Himself is too wonderful for me to grasp, too lofty for me to attain.[22] Meanwhile, O Lord Jesus, I will embrace Thee who didst become a little child for me. In my weakness I clasp Thee who didst become weak for me. A mere man, I embrace the God made man, the God who became a man as poor as I am, and came into Jerusalem seated on a humble donkey.[23] I embrace Thee, O Lord, because Thy

9

lowly state is my greatness, and Thy weakness is my strength. The foolishness of God is my wisdom.

Thy life on earth draws me as the perfume of the beloved attracts the lover.[24] They are fragrant indeed, those ointments of Thine, and they heal the sick, strengthen the weak, and gladden the sorrowing. The fragrance of Thy power draws me to follow Thee, and gives me new life by its salve. I shall follow Thee, O Lord, even though I cannot walk with Thee upon the flower-scented hills where Thy beloved spouse finds Thee,[25] nor can I enter the garden where Thy body was buried. But let my flesh be buried with Thee, dearest Lord, in that garden, for I wish to live not for myself, but only for Thee who didst deliver Thyself up for me. May I be anointed with Thee at Thy burial with the myrrh of purity, so that sin may no longer reign over my body, nor make me rot, like a diseased animal, in my own filth. To that garden Thou didst come from the cross, and so I pray that I may take up Thy cross and follow Thee. And if I wish to know how to follow Thee, Thy answer will be a question: 'How did you wander from Me?' To this I answer that it was not by walking away on my feet, but by the inconstancy of my mind. Not wishing to give my soul wholly to Thee, I kept it to myself. Hoping to be my own master, I lost possession of myself. My life became a burden, and within me I found nothing but darkness and wretchedness, fear and need. Then I said to myself: I know what I must do. I will go to my Father and tell Him that I have sinned against heaven, and before Him.[26]

The restoration of the image by love

PRIDE corrupted the image of God in us and led us away
from God, not by means of our feet but by the desires of
our hearts. We return to God by following the same path,
but in the other direction, by the exercise of these same
desires; and humility renews us in the same image in which
God created us. This is why Saint Paul calls on us to be
mentally and spiritually remade, and to be clothed in the
new self made in God's image.[27] This renewal can only
come about by fulfilling the new commandment of charity
given us by our Saviour,[28] and if the mind clothes itself in
charity, our corrupted memory and knowledge will be
given new life and new form. How few words are needed
to express the new commandment, but how much they
imply—the stripping of our old selves, the renewal of our
inner life, the reshaping of the divine image within us. Our
power to love was poisoned by the selfishness of our desires,
and stifled by lust, so that it has tended always to seek the
very depths of vicious practices. But when charity floods
the soul and warms away the numbness, love strives towards
higher and more worthy objects. It puts aside the old ways
and takes up a new life, and on flashing wings it flies to the
highest and purest Goodness which is the source of its
being.

This is what Saint Paul was trying to show the Athenians,
when he established from the books of their philosophers
the existence of one God, in whom we live and move and
have our being.[29] Paul then quoted one of their poets[30]
who said that we are God's offspring, and in the next
sentence went on to enlarge on this saying. The Apostle
was not using this quotation to prove that we are of the
same nature or substance as God, and therefore immutable,

incorruptible and eternally happy like God the Son, who was born of the Father from all eternity and is equal to the Father in all things. No, Saint Paul uses this passage from the poet Aratus to assert that we are the offspring of God because man's soul, created in God's image, can share in His wisdom and blessedness. It is charity which raises our soul towards its destiny, but it is self-centred desire which drags it down to the things towards which, without God's help, it would most certainly be drawn.

8

Charity and Cupidity

THE only power of our soul which is equally capable of charity and cupidity is the one we call love, and when charity is newly poured into the soul among the surviving traces of long-standing lust, that power finds itself divided into warring factions. Saint Paul is speaking of this internal division when he says *I do that which I will not*,[31] and when he tells the Galatians that the desires of the flesh contend against those of the spirit.[32] This is the conflict which makes it impossible for a man to do all that his will desires. But we must observe here that Saint Paul is not speaking of two contrary natures with this *flesh* and this *spirit*. The Manichees thought that he was speaking of two natures, but in fact he uses the word *spirit* to designate the newness of soul resulting from the inpouring of charity, the charity of God with which the Holy Spirit floods our hearts. By *flesh* he means the unhappy slavery to which our souls are shackled by the remains of bad habits. These terms he uses to show that within our souls there is a ceaseless conflict between our deeply rooted habits and the new presence of charity.

Free will, and the choice between good and evil

THE flesh lusts against the spirit and the spirit against the flesh, as Saint Paul says, but when Saint John speaks of the concupiscence of the flesh,[33] he does not mean that all evil desires are caused by the flesh, for the devils in hell are ruled by evil desires even though they have no flesh. He simply means that these desires come from man and not from God. Indeed, throughout Holy Scripture, man is designated by the word 'flesh'. In the soul there is, on the one hand, concupiscence or cupidity, and on the other, charity, which belongs to the spirit of God since it is poured into our hearts by the Holy Spirit. Now between these two poles lies free will, so that whichever of its two main appetites the soul may decide to follow, it does so by virtue of its free will. But this does not mean, as some foolishly claim, that free will gives man the ability to do good or evil equally, for, left to himself, man cannot even formulate so much as a thought as coming from himself. It is God alone who brings it about that by our free will we wish to do something and then put the wish into effect. The thing that counts is God's mercy, not our will or our effort.

But surely, it might be objected, this would make it seem as if there were no power of free will in man at all. To this I would answer that free will is a power of the soul, or of human nature, if you wish, by means of which we consent to something in the light of the judgement of our reason. Free will is not itself the consent to this or that good or evil thing. It is simply that by which our consent is given. Consent is an action. Free will is a power which brings about the action of consent, when we have made the judgement as to whether our consent shall be given. In this process, consent comes from the will, and judgement from the reason. Will and reason together constitute free will. The function of reason is to propose for our choice good and evil, right and wrong, and whatever may lie between these extremes. The will consents to one or other of the alternatives proposed, but consent always implies that there is freedom to choose or not to choose, to approve or disapprove. When we will something good, it is not laid down from the start, as it were, by our free will. Whether we will good or evil, we do not lose the freedom of our wills, any more than we lose the use of our reason, our judgement or our liberty. God works in us the power to will, but this does not mean that we lose the power of willing. It is only by God's grace that we can use our reason well, but this need not stop us from using our reason. All the good we do derives from God, but that is no cause for ceasing to do good actions. We are of ourselves unable to think so much as one thought, since our sufficiency is of God, but God's sufficiency is ample for us. All that we do is done with the help of God's grace, but it is none the less done with our will and our reason. Therefore, we do nothing except of our own free will.[34]

10

Charity is all-perfect

FOR my part I can say that my soul has already had enough of sin without wallowing in it any further, and I can learn a valuable lesson from the sight of evil-doers whose scheming and sinning eventually recoil upon their heads. There is no reward in sin, and if anyone finds any satisfaction in evil, it is hard to think what form this satisfaction takes.

There is indeed no comparison between satiety in wickedness and the hunger of charity which leads to the fulfilment of all our deepest desires, and brings us to the completest joy and delight. Even more difficult is it to imagine any shade of comparison between the blessedness to be found in heaven and the emptiness of the dubious pleasures of sin. For the more a man strives to satisfy his longings and the desires of his bodily appetites, the more he is starving himself of the food of true values. He may be the richest and most successful man in the world, but in reality he is worse off than a beggar in the gutter.

Evil men may plot their wicked deeds on every side, but in the midst of it all my soul must be completely detached; it must put itself so completely in God's hands that both its life and death are surrendered to Him who lived, died and rose again for us. In no other way but by drinking deep of this saving draught will my mind reel and my soul thereafter slumber in delightful repose. And so my love for God, with all my heart, soul and strength, would have no place for my own interests, but only for those of Christ. And before the warmth of my love for my fellow men all self-centredness would melt away, so that my every thought and aim would be focused on them.

Charity—a short word indeed, but with its meaning of perfect and unalloyed love it sums up the whole of man's attitude to God and His creatures; or, to use Our Lord's own explanation, it is on charity that all the law and the prophets depend.[35] Surely for us, then, there can be no need to demand great signs and miracles as the Jews were wont to do. For charity gives the soul a spiritual circumcision quite unlike that ordered for men's bodies by the Old Law. And the delights of a never-ending Sabbath, the saving victims offered by the loving soul to God, the perfumed incense and fragrant smoke of sacrifice—these are merely some of the fruits of charity when it is firmly rooted in the soul. Yet none can flourish or even live in a soul where charity is not present.

Charity is spiritual circumcision

THE circumcision effected in the soul by charity has little in common with the circumcision of men's bodies, for it is the complete sloughing off of our baser inclinations as they affect both body and soul. The result is that the flames of lust are quenched and anger's heat is cooled. Tempering also the appetites of gluttony, charity further roots out all envy and banishes completely the mother of all vices, pride. And it so soothes the sting of melancholy in the soul that even accidie, that spiritual torpor which is the aftermath of melancholy, is waylaid. Yet another effect of charity's circumcision of the soul is that munificence cuts the shackles of graspingness so that nothing—least of all the desire for wealth—can take God's place in the soul's devotion.

Surely no physical operation could have greater effect than this spiritual circumcision which amputates vice, drains the pus of sin, removes the dead skin of original sin and burns away the gangrene of long-standing evil. Then the mind is untroubled by fear or worry, for the calm of perfect love reigns there. Lust's evil desires can leave no stain; anger's raging will never again sear the soul, nor will pride inflate it with self-importance. Gone is the blinding desire for earthly glory together with the heat of anger and the sting of ambition. No longer does the soul yearn for masses of worldly wealth; no more can sadness make it downcast nor envy gnaw at it. For as Saint Paul tells us, when charity reigns in the soul, there is no envy or double-dealing, no arrogance or self-centredness, no self-pity or self-aggrandizement.[36]

It is easy to see, then, that the circumcision of the soul destroys all evil at the same time as purifying all the senses of the body, just as the surgeon's knife cores out a poisoned

wound. Thus the eyes no longer roam in search of excite-
ment in every object; words of evil no longer make ears
prick up; the palate no longer craves for exotic flavours,
the tongue no longer delights in the foulest conversation;
touch and smell no longer yearn for softness and fragrance.

12

Charity, the true Sabbath of the soul

CHARITY brings with it a Sabbath very unlike that known
to the Jews of old. No idea of what it is can be possessed
by those weighed down by sin, for in the shackles of their
passions they could taste next to nothing of its delight. If
only Pharaoh's taskmasters would allow me a mere half-
hour to enjoy the silent calm of this Sabbath, my soul would
straightway slumber in its perfect peace—a peace that no
king in his palace could experience even with the aid of
limitless wealth. For a wretched sinner such as I, it seems
ridiculous to hope for this Sabbath, but seek and hope for
it I shall.

And if, Lord, Thou dost heed my desire and lead me out
of the mire of sin's pit, grant that I may learn by even the
slightest experience that for the God-fearing a reward of
greatest delight is in store.[37] Such things are revealed only
to those who love Thee, and those who love Thee find rest
in Thee in that true calm and peace which is the Sabbath of
the soul.

What reason had the Jews for resting on the Sabbath day
apart from the fact that God rested from the work of creation on the seventh day? But this seems to imply that God
did not rest on the other six days because He was busy with
the work of creation. Hence the command to do nothing
on the seventh day. But if the Jewish Sabbath had the effect

17

of leaving their souls in a state of perfect openness to God—
as indeed it should—they would see that Jesus is God, and
the veil of disbelief would fall from their eyes to show them
how the perfect celebration of the Sabbath is found in
charity. The ritual Sabbath meals would have no further
part to play in their lives, since in God's own dwelling-place
a delighted cry would burst from their lips and a song of
rejoicing would be heard. They would sing of how they
rejoice and make merry because God has embraced their
souls more thrillingly than any wine.[38] And at the peak of
their happiness they would cry out with the prophet that
all their delight was to be found in God, whose Saviour
completed their joy.[39]

13

The seventh day

BUT what, we may ask, is so special about the seventh day
of creation? After all, the work of the first day—the
creation of light and the banishment of darkness—was
apparently just as wonderful. Equally marvellous was the
creation of the firmament on the second day to divide the
waters of the earth from those of the heavens. To collect
the waters of the earth into one place, and then to carpet
the dry land with flowers and grass and to beautify it with
trees and fruit on the third day—could any work be greater
than this? But no one would be so foolish as to claim that
the fourth day's work of creating the sun, moon and stars
to divide day from night and measure time was anything
less magnificent. Yet easily comparable with this was the
production from the waters of living things and winged
things that fly above the earth, as happened on the fifth day.
Was this greater or less than the work of the sixth day when

the land yielded the different kinds of living creatures—cattle, creeping things, wild beasts and so on—and man was formed from clay and given life and soul by the divine breath?

But in spite of their marvels, none of the days of creation, it seems to me, can be compared with the seventh day on which no work was done and God rested after completing His handiwork. *And on the seventh day*, the book of Genesis tells us, *God ended His work which He had made: and He rested on the seventh day from all His work which He had done.*[40] Here we are told the two requirements of the Sabbath: it must be a day, and at the same time there is to be rest. This seventh day, however, does not seem to me to be measured by the time between sunrise and sunset, to be bright in the morning and dusk in the evening. For the first day of creation described in the Bible is not in fact called 'the first day', but *one day*.[41] And the difficulty is that the following day is called by the author *the second day*, and therefore the preceding one must have been the first day. It would be easy enough if at the end of the account of each phase of creation we read of the passing of 'one day' up to a total of six times, but whatever solution may be proposed the text is clear: *And there was evening and morning one day.... And the evening and morning were the second day.*[42] These words seem to me to imply that created things are always in a state of change—beginning and ending, succeeding and failing, to name but a few manifestations of their changeability. The seventh day, however, is the exception to this rule, since there is no mention made of its beginning or end, of its morning or evening.

This means that the day of God's rest is not bound by time, but is eternal. No doubt, the picture in your mind was of God performing His handiwork within the context of time and taking a rest within the same context, as if worn out by the exertion of creation—not so much an idea of

God as the picture of an idol, if you will allow me to say so. For although we should never dream of worshipping an idol in a temple, we may easily fall into the trap of unconsciously doing so in our hearts. Contrary to what you may have thought, creation involved no exertion for God, since *He spoke and they were made*, as the Psalmist says.[43] Neither did God rest on only one of the seven days, since the day of His resting is eternal, as I have shown, and His resting and His eternity are one and the same. Your imagination had conjured up a picture of God in your own image, and so it seemed to you that creation was God's way of making good the lack of something to delight His gaze, or of something to give Him the satisfaction of achievement. Precisely because nothing is wanting to God, the Bible does not speak of Him as finding satisfaction in created things, but shows that creation was the result of the outpouring of His love. His act of creation, indeed, brought all things into being, and they are kept in being until led to their end in accordance with His plan. But God does not *have* to do this; rather He wills to do so, with the result that His all-powerful majesty holds sway over the whole earth, and every single thing manifests His plan. Yet in spite of His ruling and ordering all things, He is always at rest in His overflowing love, His everlasting and never-changing Sabbath.

Love is His only reason for creating, guiding and planning all things from beginning to end, and that is why we read of His rest at the end of the story of creation. His love, it should be obvious by now, is the same as His will and goodness—in fact, it is His very being. And while the succession of the days of creation with their mornings and evenings makes us think of the change involved in the state of creaturehood, in the same way this day without predecessor or successor, without compare, without beginning or end, puts us in mind of God's eternity and of the rest and satisfaction that were not the outcome of exertion and need.

And now another problem must be faced and answered: what is the meaning behind the numbers six and seven in the story of creation?

14

God's work and rest

IN my opinion six is the perfect number because, when added together, its factors total the number itself: one plus two plus three equals six; six ones make six, twice three is six, three twos are six, the number having no other factors. It is fitting, then, that there were six days of creation, because, like the number six, God's creation was all-perfect and contained nothing superfluous.

The number seven is kept for God's rest at the conclusion of his handiwork, and we have already seen how God's resting and His love are one and the same. And Our Lord tells us that the Father loves the Son and discloses to Him all that He does,[44] and that it is because He keeps His Father's commandments that He lives on in His love.[45] The Father for His part points to His beloved Son in whom He is well pleased.[46] Now the delight that the Father and Son take in each other is nothing else than their mutual love and embrace in which each rests in the other. This is the one thing that belongs to them both, or rather it is in this that they are one. And the delight and joy which they take in each other is called the Holy Spirit, because He is common to the Father and Son by proceeding from both of them, being consubstantial with them.

Yet Holy Writ often speaks of the Spirit as being seven-fold, although He is indeed only one Spirit and is one with the Father and Son. The reason for this description is that from His fullness there flows a sevenfold grace. For instance, the prophet saw a stone bearing seven eyes,[47] and Saint John's vision showed him seven spirits before the throne of God.[48] And in conclusion I may say that this should suffice to show the excellence of charity, in which the creator and ruler of all things celebrates an everlasting Sabbath.

15

Charity's mark in every creature

IF you were to look at every creature from the beginning of creation to the end of time—whether it were the most radiant angel or the tiniest worm—you would see in it signs of God's goodness and His overflowing love. Yet to speak of God's love as overflowing might lead to the idea of space and movement being involved, whereas His love contains all things within itself in such a way that all opposites are reconciled in His perfect unchangingness. Thus in the order established by God everything has a place and purpose, and nothing mars the beauty of His plan or disturbs the peace and harmony of all creation. And so if anything tries to break away from the place in creation established for it by God, it is trying to usurp God's power to itself. Whatever happens, however, it cannot disturb the harmony of God's creation, but rather it enhances it by comparison with its own instability, ugliness and evil. For it is a fact of the order of nature that everything seeks its own fore-ordained place and will brook no opposing force. For instance, if a stone is thrown into the air, it soon reverses its course and falls earthwards as if forced down again, and then, only because it encounters the contrary force of some solid surface, does it come to rest. Or, to take another example, oil when mixed with water always rises to the top where it floats on the surface. Each thing, then, has its natural place—even trees and plants, as we can see from the fact that some flourish and bear fruit better in soft ground, rocky soil, clay or sand as the case may be, which has been proved by experiments in transplantation.

Every solid object, too, is made up of parts which are joined together by a bond of unity to form the whole. And nature has so arranged that, if any of these parts are disturbed from their proper place and function, the unity and harmony of the whole are upset until the parts are replaced. And, to take just one last example to illustrate my point, notice how animals naturally seek to preserve their safety and well-being and to satisfy their appetites, for when they have done these things they have fulfilled all their desires and can be at peace. For since they are not endowed with the powers of reason and knowledge, their desires are limited to the demands of their bodies.

16

The desire for perfect happiness

THE outstanding characteristic of the soul of man, which no other living thing shares, is that it strives towards higher things by leaving on one side the allurements presented by the senses of the body. This striving is satisfied only after a long but pleasant search, when the highest and best object is reached. And below this standard lies wretchedness, no matter how pleasant or lofty it may seem. It is a state of wretchedness because there is still something lacking, something that you seek and yearn for, since you have not yet found that perfect happiness to which the soul is naturally drawn in much the same way as iron is attracted to a loadstone.

That all men desire happiness is an undeniable fact witnessed by the inner convictions and conscience of all, and until it is found a man is restless and unsatisfied. What a pity, then, that men should be so blind and perverse as to seek this perfect happiness and yet not take any steps to attain it, simply because they act in a way conducive to unhappiness. In my opinion men do this under the misleading influence of a false picture of happiness, and so devote their energies to avoiding poverty, sadness, hunger and thirst. Often, in fact, the misfortunes which they try to evade are the very means by which the everlasting happiness of heaven is found, as Our Lord Himself said in the sermon on the mount: *Blessed are ye poor, for yours is the Kingdom of God. Blessed are they that mourn, for they shall be comforted. Blessed are ye that hunger now, for you shall be filled.*[49] Poverty, therefore, has riches for its reward, with everlasting joy taking the place of the sadness and misfortunes of this world, and hunger's pangs being banished for ever.

Obviously, perfect happiness means that riches, joy and satisfaction are present, but because a sham happiness can divert the efforts of the will into wrong channels, the satisfaction of an evil man's desires may bring him a certain counterfeit pleasure. Little does he realize what consolation is in store for God's special friends, who may have to live a life of difficulty and trouble in this world, or what joy is engendered by hope. Any outward appearance of unhappiness fills him with fear, and so he snatches at whatever he *thinks* will bring him happiness, because he does not realize that in the true scale of values wretchedness in this world will be rewarded by unceasing joy in heaven.

To behave like this is as ludicrous as for a sick man, who yearns to be well again, to refuse amputation or cauterization in favour of poultices, which seem to soothe but actually encourage the disease. Drastic measures are all that will help him, but yet he deceives himself into using more pleasant remedies which will not bring him the happiness of recovery. This is because he is thinking only in terms of his present comfort in a vain search for health and happiness; but clearly he will go from bad to worse and never find the satisfaction of the cure that he seeks. This example clearly illustrates how ridiculous it is for the soul, which is equal to the angels and inferior only to God, to seek its satisfaction in things that are beneath it.

17

The desire for health and riches

IT is sad to see how the soul, which is second only to God, degrades itself. It will love the world, although it is a more wonderful creation than the world. The glory of the sun will arouse its envious admiration, in spite of the fact that its beauty leaves the sun in shadow. Men will discuss and search into the stars and planets, yet forget that their souls are on a level far above the constellations. Searching into the secrets of creation, they neglect the fact that their soul is the greatest of all secrets. And they are full of questions about the things around them without ever concentrating their thoughts on themselves. By all means let them discuss and analyse such things, but not to the extent of becoming enamoured of them, or of calling God's wisdom into doubt.

Man's love and consideration should rather be focused on Him who has placed him so high in the order of creation, not so that man may find his happiness in things inferior to him, but so that all things may contribute to the honour of his high status and God alone be his reward in the unending joy of heaven. It is madness to pursue the fleeting beauty of this world when the soul's beauty never ages or coarsens, and when sickness or death cannot lessen it or take it away. No, happiness is not to be sought in this direction, for it is to be found only where there is nothing left to wish for. Nor is there any use in looking for physical health to provide peace and satisfaction, since great effort must be devoted to the curing of sickness, and even then a cruel death may be brought about by a devastating disease. When healthy, we give much time and care to the preservation of our body's good condition to ward off plague and sickness, forgetting that death is inevitable.

Some people think that perhaps peace and security are to be found in wealth. But they have to toil to amass a fortune, they worry about keeping it for fear that they may lose it, and they are in the depths of sorrow when it melts away. The more money they have, the more they have grounds for fear: fear of the rich man who may swindle, fear of the robber who may steal, fear of the servant who may mismanage. And so often men hoard their riches to their own disadvantage, as the wise man said long ago.[50] In the long run the poor have much more peace, for robbers do not lie in wait for empty-handed travellers, as the proverb puts it. There is no point in the poor man locking his door at night, since he has no reason to fear burglars. On the other hand, the rich man's cares plague him every minute of the day, while at night he suffers the penalty of high living with an indigestion that keeps him awake. How different he is from the bride in the Canticle whose heart is wakeful while she sleeps;[51] or from the psalmist who sleeps so peacefully as soon as his head touches the pillow![52] For them the senses of the body are deadened, worries about the passing day are banished, and the soul rests in God's own peace, as it tastes and sees the sweetness of the Lord and learns the happiness of those who place their trust in Him.

There is no comparison between this and the restless slumbers of a man always on the lookout for more wealth, with the insatiable ambition to have everything in his possession. This is Solomon's meaning when he says: *A covetous man will not be satisfied with money, and he who loves riches shall reap no fruit from them.*[53] And on those who hoard up what is not their own, the prophet's curse is pronounced, when he describes those piles of gold and silver as so much mud in which a man will stick and be sucked down.[54]

18

Saints and sinners among the rich

NOTICE well that, according to Solomon's words, it is not he who *has* riches, but he who *loves* riches that will reap no fruit from them. This shows that holiness and riches are not contradictory if there is no love of wealth for its own sake, or if it is not sought as the be-all and end-all of life. Holy men may well be rich if they remember the Apostle's warning not to have a high opinion of themselves nor to place all their hopes in wealth.[55] Instead they can easily store up for themselves a sure foundation for the true life of eternity by sharing their fortune with the needy. For they will see their riches bear ample fruit when they are welcomed as the blessed sons of the Father, because when Christ was hungry they gave Him to eat.[56] And because they realize that the desire for riches is a snare of the devil, as Saint Paul puts it,[57] they do not devote all their efforts to amassing wealth, and therefore they are not worried about its possible loss. They know full well that Our Lord has promised that God will provide them with what is necessary, so that there is no need to be anxious about what to eat or drink, but rather they must seek first the Kingdom of God and His justice, and then all those things will be theirs without the asking.[58] And if in the end they lose their wealth, it is no cause for sadness but rather for joy, since it impresses on them even more that a higher and more lasting good is waiting for them, as the Apostle promises.[59]

With sinners it is quite another story, for they imagine that a fortune will satisfy the yearnings of the soul which can be content only with the possession of God. But in fact all their wealth does not do them much good, since it calls for effort and worry, with the sad result that they become blind to all but money. This is a bad enough fate indeed to suffer in this life, but what will become of them in the next? Scripture tells us how they will groan with remorse at having travelled wearily through the deserts and rocky paths of sin. God meant quite another path for them, but they missed it, and now they see that their pride and ostentation have brought them no advantage, for it was all as fleeting as a shadow and has disappeared with the speed of a post-horse. They were born and they died, leaving as little trace as a ship when its wake has vanished, since by devoting themselves to evil they left not even the memory of a life well lived. Such are the thoughts of the sinners in hell, whose evil life engenders no hope in them more lasting than wind-blown dust and storm-tossed spray. They are as quickly forgotten as the overnight guest who never comes again.[60]

What other conclusion may we draw, then, than that the perfect rest of the soul's Sabbath cannot be found in health or riches?

19

The instability of worldly friendships

To some people it seems that perfect peace and stability are to be found in loving and being loved, and there is no denying this on condition that the love is rooted in God and is for God's sake. For such a love is important and is to be encouraged. But friendships based on worldly values or rooted in lust give rise to nothing but envy, suspicion and jealousy which drive away all peace from the soul. And even if such effects do not follow, death must inevitably break the bond of friendship—much to the sorrow of the one left on earth. Then in its wake death will bring cruel punishment to those who have misused the gift of friendship. The love experienced by the good in friendship we shall discuss elsewhere,[61] but let us never forget that it has been known for the bitterest hatred to arise between the closest friends.[62]

20

The perfection and pre-eminence of charity

To see ourselves as being more wonderful than any other part of creation is the most delightful and honourable of all satisfactions, for if we stand on the lofty heights of a clear conscience, the whole world is under our feet, there being no sin to shackle us to things on a lower level than ourselves. Because of this realization no man and no thing can stir us to fear or envy, since our only desires are directed to God. Such a dignity as ours can never be taken from us, and no evil done to us can cause us any grief or worry. The gaze of our soul being directed upwards to that inheritance in heaven which never spoils or fades, we look down on worldly wealth as corruptible, on fleshly desires as poisonous to the soul, and on worldly pride as passing. And thus with the prophet we rejoice to think that mortal things are like grass and wither just as quickly; but the word of the Lord endures for ever.[63]

The imagination would fail to find any greater joy or any deeper peace than we feel in freedom from the violent surgings of passion, from the smouldering flames of lust, and from all the allurements that beset us on every side. Instead of our being disturbed by such things, the dew of modesty has cooled the heat of our bodies, bringing them under the sway of the spirit, away from the attraction of physical pleasure, so that now the body becomes a most willing helper in the soul's striving towards God. In this way we come close to sharing the tranquil rest of God when insults have no effect on us, when persecutions or penalties have no terror for us, when prosperity or adversity have no influence on us, and when friend and enemy share the same measure of our consideration. This is indeed to resemble closely *Him who maketh His sun to rise upon the good and bad, and raineth upon the just and the unjust.*[64]

For all these things are rooted and done in charity, and in charity only, which brings with it true peace and delight, since charity is the Lord's yoke. And we know that if we answer Our Lord's call and bear His yoke, our souls will find rest, since His yoke is sweet and His burden light.[65]

Saint Paul describes charity as patient and kind, feeling no envy or pride, and never being perverse or insolent.[66] He says this because the other virtues help us as a carriage bears the weary traveller upon his way, as marching rations strengthen the tired soldier, as a light shows the road by night, or as arms help in winning a battle. But charity, which all men must have in conjunction with the other virtues, is in a special way the tired man's rest, the traveller's shelter, the voyager's destination, and the victor's trophy.

This we realize when we compare it with the other virtues. For faith draws us to our native land, while hope gives us strength and sustenance for the journey through life's hardships, our arms for the struggle being provided by temperance, prudence, fortitude and justice. And when the outcome of death is perfect charity in the vision of God, faith, which was the preparation for that vision, will have no further place, because when we see God in perfect love there is no longer any need to believe in Him, as it were, from afar. And when we embrace God in the arms of our love, hope will play no part, since there is nothing further to hope for. Temperance wages its war against lust, prudence against error, fortitude against adversity, and justice against injustice.

But where charity is present, there is also perfect chastity and thus no lust for temperance to combat; there is the happiest satisfaction with no adversity for fortitude to fight; there is no injustice for justice to withstand, for all things are now reconciled in perfect peace and harmony. Yet faith loses all its character of virtue unless its belief is based on love, and for hope to be a virtue it must love its object. Similarly by seeing all virtues from the aspect of charity, we realize that temperance is merely love unmotivated by lust, that prudence is love not misled by error, that fortitude is love withstanding all adversity, and justice a love that brings under its sway every form of injustice. Faith, then, we must conclude, is the starting point of perfect love, which is exercised and manifested in all the other virtues. But the perfection of love is found in charity alone.

21

The days of creation and the virtues

For our souls, faith is like the first day of creation, when the spheres of light and darkness were divided, since those with the true faith have been singled out from the unbelievers. The second day may have the virtue of hope assigned to it for, just as the sky was made by God to separate the waters above from those below, we whose true home is in heaven and who hope for heaven as the reward of our faith, have been separated by God from those whose interests are focused only upon this world, even in what they ask of God.

On the third day God commanded the dry land to appear, and this may be compared to the work of temperance in us who mortify our earth-bound bodies and restrain within their necessary limits the salt waters of fleshly desires, so that the dry land of our heart appears and thirsts for its Lord and God. The fourth day shows us the division of day from night in the same way as prudence shows us how to distinguish between what we may and may not do. With its help the light of wisdom bursts forth with the brightness of the newly-made sun, and knowledge of the things of the spirit begins to shine like the moon, waxing or waning with our growth or decrease in holiness. With this knowledge of spiritual things the soul learns to look up to the example of holy men of past ages as if they were shining stars, and to discover the difference between those before or after the giving of the Law, and those before or after Christ's earning of grace for man, just as the lights from heaven mark the difference between days and years, hours and months.

The virtue of fortitude is like the fifth day of creation, for by it we are able to endure the storms of the great and spreading sea of the world in which we live. On that day were created fishes and birds, and so by fortitude God enables us to remain alive and not to drown in the waves and storms of temptation. And as our souls strive longingly for the things of heaven and experience even now a foretaste of eternity's gifts, we increase and multiply with a progeny of good works, fulfilling in our souls the command given to the newly-created birds. Then on the sixth day were created the beasts and cattle and things creeping on the earth, and this part of creation may be compared to the virtue of justice. For now that the divine likeness clothes us again, we can, in virtue of our reformed nature, command the savage beasts of vice and passion, and subdue our body by the soul's dictates, submitting our soul to none but God. The work of justice is then completed, for there is rendered to everything merely what is its due. This is man's privilege, belonging neither to birds nor to serpents.

The story of creation has, then, many lessons to teach us, allowing us in this examination to cull from it many fruitful ideas for the life of the soul. We have read of God's blessing on the birds and fishes which was not shared by the beasts or serpents, and how by God's blessing they increased and multiplied in the sea and in the air. But notice that there was no blessing and no command given to the beasts. From this we may draw the lesson that virtues and holy desires—which we have just compared to the fishes and birds created on the fifth day—are blessed by God so that they increase and grow strong by being brought to birth in our souls. And just as to man, created in the image and likeness of God, was given the blessing of domination over the beasts, so too when righteousness and justice have been rewarded by the restoration of the divine likeness in the soul, the rule of God brings under its sway the spiritual beasts of which the psalmist speaks. *Deliver not up to beasts the souls that confess to Thee,*[67] he prayed, for the beasts of vice and passion must not be allowed to multiply within us.

But what about the seventh day, the Sabbath that saw the completion of God's handiwork? To us the Sabbath brings perfect rest when the work of all the virtues is completed. And this completion of their work is found in charity, which affords refreshment for our souls and the perfect attuning of our lives to God. With charity as their root all the virtues grow to perfection, until on the seventh day charity refreshes us with God's grace. And here yet another useful image from the book of Genesis[68] can be applied to charity by calling it the seventh month, when the ark of

33

our soul comes to a gentle rest after the long flood of temptation.

But above all, we must remember its relation to the other virtues; temperance is its servant, prudence its watchdog, fortitude its sword, and justice its attentive companion.

22

The other virtues in relation to charity

THE task of temperance, then, is to subdue and restrain the wayward inclinations of both body and soul, lest we misguidedly prefer the pleasures of the bodily appetites to the delightful love of God and neighbour. Prudence is present to distinguish between what should and should not be the object of our love, for otherwise our desires, shamming as true charity, may run away with our rather reckless hearts. And fortitude withstands worldly misfortunes only to keep the soul from falling into excessive love or pity for itself when things do not turn out as we wish, or when difficulties beset us on every side.

It is clear, then, from their connection with charity that temperance, prudence and fortitude may be called virtues only if they are used to help in the finding and keeping of charity. Therefore we cannot say that temperance is a virtue if, while curbing the desires of our animal nature, it does not at the same time bridle the wanton soul which yearns for wealth and power on the pretext of loving itself in conformity with charity. Nor will that prudence be worthy of the name of virtue which teaches a man to make false judgements about what should and should not be the object of our love, or about what is truly a loss or a gain of worldly goods, for obviously a man misled in this way will so lack charity that he will pursue his own advantage to the ruination of others. And who would ever grace Catiline's bravery with the name of virtue, when, in spite of helping him to bear difficulties and reverses in an almost superhuman way, it enabled him to secure the booty of his own pleasure—though not, admittedly, of power in this world—and thus deprived him of virtue's reward? For we should say that whatever is not rooted in charity, can have no connection with it, even though the man thirsting for worldly acclaim and glory may live frugally, or the quick-witted trickster have a reputation for prudence, or the Stoic have schooled himself to be insensitive to all hardship. We might put it another way by saying that the Ark of our soul, like Noah's Ark, is measured in cubits, and if one cubit of charity is lacking in its overall measurements, the whole structure will be faulty. And so true temperance ensures that no allurements misguide genuine prudence, for under such a misleading influence the soul could be misdirected by reason to go beyond the basic laws of charity.

Perfect love finally brings its devotees to calm rest, and refreshes them with its delightful sweetness. But this can happen only when the body's death has finally conquered the allurements of the flesh, when the vision of God's own brightness has banished the darkness of error, and when the reverses of this world have been exchanged for the security of heaven. Then, and only then, can charity lay aside the arms of the virtues which it used throughout the battle of life, when the other virtues overflow into the fullness of charity and become so absorbed into it that they are in-distinguishable from it. No physical attractions can ever tempt its chastity now; no error can ever mar its brightness; no adversity can cow its strength.

This has been promised to us by God when He told Moses that He would banish all ravenous beasts from among His people so that they could sleep safely.[69] For when the land of our bodies has been rid of the savage beasts of passion, God lulls us into a heavenly sleep. And then the sea of God's brightness swallows us up in its vastness and carries us outside our own small compass, so that we see that the Lord is God.

This is the celebration of that Sabbath in heaven which will go on, as Isaias tells us, for month after month, and for Sabbath after Sabbath.[70] And when, one Sabbath, we have tasted as much of the initial stages of charity as the day allows, we shall be carried outside the bustle of this world into that unmarred Sabbath which no trouble can disturb and no bodily misfortune can hamper. Then, and only then, shall we love the Lord our God with all our heart and strength and by means of every virtue, and our neighbour as ourselves.[71]

Render, therefore, to all men their due: tribute to whom tribute is due: fear to whom fear: honour to whom honour, Saint Paul tells us,[72] meaning that justice kindles charity into a burning fire after it had begun by harming no one and grown by being agreeable to all men. This is noticeable in anyone who, by always wishing for the good of others, easily wins their affection. Such a man cannot possibly offend anyone by his gentle way of life, which manifests itself in obedience to superiors in fear and reverence, in harmony with his equals in a respectful consideration, and in a humble opinion of himself before those below him which is based on sympathy and understanding.

Those who realize the reward of charity are also influenced in their dealings with money matters, for in accordance with the Apostle's command[73] they do not delay payment of their debts until forced to satisfy their impatient exactors, but rather they cheerfully pay up even before the request is made. And since even the management of money comes within the scope of charity, we may safely say that the peace of perfect love will embrace every facet of our lives, so that in the light of it the decision about our eternal reward or punishment will be made. For the rules of eternal justice based on charity dictate that we fulfil perfectly the command to grant every man his due, which we do by loving the proper objects of love in the measure that they should be loved. In other words, we are to love God more than ourselves, and our fellow men as ourselves, loving God only for God's sake and ourselves and our neighbour for no other reason than God.

This, I trust, makes it absolutely clear that perfect justice depends on perfect charity, since justice may be defined as love directed to its proper object. And progress in this virtue is marked by an ever deepening peace and satisfaction in the soul, which God alone can give.[74]

PART II

I

Recapitulation of Part One

IN the first part of this work we came to the agreement that the highest virtue is to be found in the perfection of charity. And indeed we cannot conceive of any virtue that does not take its rise from charity, any more than we can conceive of any perfect work which does not have its consummation in charity. For in charity we find both the fullness of the Old Law and the perfection of the gospel. In charity we see the spiritual circumcision of a whole human nature, both internal and external, which is the true Sabbath rest of our souls.

We have already proved that this Sabbath rest can be ours only in charity, for charity is the light burden and the easy yoke which our Saviour in His mercy offers to each one of us. *You will find*, He says, *rest for your souls*.[1] But we have also observed that this yoke is not laid on our shoulders without some irksomeness ensuing for our fallen nature. And therefore I was about to enter into some detail on the subject of the three lusts of our fallen state that Saint John enumerates—the lust of the eyes, the lust of the flesh, and the pride of life.[2] It is on the analysis of these three immoderate desires that he bases the whole of his concept of cupidity. However, the death of my friend Simon came as an interruption to the work that I had in hand, and since it has taken me a little time to recover from the loss of so great a friend, it seems best for me to begin this again with a slightly different consideration, namely the one that Saint

Paul offers us when he says that cupidity is the root of all evils.[3]

Cupidity is the exact opposite of charity, which is the root of all virtues. And this means that as long as the root of cupidity is fixed in our hearts, however much we may hack away at the shoots it puts out, others will surely take their place until such time as the root is gone for good and all. In this connection I am not, of course, speaking of those whose vices are obvious and flagrant, and who make little attempt to be anything but vicious. But I am speaking of those who labour seriously at the profession of being Christ's followers, who examine their consciences to the very depths, and spare themselves nothing of the truth of self-knowledge.

2

The soul's effort

THE labour involved, however, is not the sweated labour of physical exertion, but rather it is an effort of the soul, for, like the soul's Sabbath of which we have already spoken, it is on the spiritual level. Naturally the effort of the inner man directs the outward actions, which are unlikely to take place without it. To realize this, think of hunters and fowlers who go to such lengths of physical endeavour because the chase fills them with inward pleasure. Think of the apostles who were proud to suffer something for the love of Christ while yet they suffered in prisons and chains. Think of all those who indulge in thoroughly unworthy occupations—adulterers who will suffer anything to satisfy the pleasure of lust, thieves who take no thought of physical risk while their minds are on their haul. For when we think of these we see that the outward sufferings of the body give no trouble to the soul. And whatever happens outwardly remains outward, without touching the inner man at all.

Why is it, then, that one man will rejoice and another will grumble when the same sort of food is put before both of them? Why is it that two men, smitten by the same sort of wound, will react so differently—the one behaving as if he were half dead, and the other looking, if anything, more cheerful than ever? Why is it that poverty, necessity and misfortune affect different people in completely different ways, to the extent that some will praise God and others will curse Him for what He has allowed to happen to them? For both have the same spectacle of misfortune to contemplate, but whereas one remains undisturbed, the other is moved to many ill-judged actions. Again, when the chance of attaining some longed-for ambition is made remote, some men are so consumed by the lust for power that there is no crime too base for them to commit, if it will be the means of their reaching the desired objective. Other men, on the contrary, entirely innocent of this vice, will accept things as they happen and make no fuss at all.

3

Peace from charity

SIMILARLY, the same thing may happen to any two bodies with completely different effects, depending on the individual's state of health. For some the effect may be agreeable, while others may find it just the opposite. Thus the food that one man eats to his harm, is beneficial to another's health; and the sun, which destroys the sight of a man with weak eyes, increases the pleasure of a man with good strong eyes. In fact, in the bodily sphere, things work out to the advantage or disadvantage of the body entirely according to the *inner* state of the man, and in the same way the external accidents of fortune are received by men's minds according to what is already in their souls, so that some will be troubled and others will be unaffected. And obviously, the man who is joined to God with perfect charity, is the one who will be least disturbed by the external accidents of fortune, since his mind is perfectly at peace. Far from allowing himself to be upset, he realizes that everything that happens to him is for some use, some purpose in his spiritual life.

A man who is bound to the yoke of cupidity, on the other hand, will think himself as well off as the man beneath the yoke of charity, so long as nothing happens to disturb the peace of his soul. But as soon as something happens to arouse his anger, his passions come away like so many wild beasts, rushing out from the secret caverns of his soul to tear him to pieces.

It is only when we throw off the yoke of cupidity that we find how very easy, by comparison with our former load, is the burden which Christ lays upon our shoulders— a burden so light, so joyous that it lifts us up from the ground instead of weighing us down. Indeed, it raises us up from earth to heaven. If, then, we would have our share in all the joy and peace that Christ desires for us, we must look diligently into all the things that cause us disquiet, and into all the troubles that our vices cause us. We must dig down and strike with a strong, sharp thrust—not flabbily or with a blunted axe—if we are to get to the roots of all that is evil in us.

The threefold concupiscence

IF we investigate thoroughly, I think we shall see that all our troubles arise from the lust of the flesh, the lust of the eyes, or the pride of life.[4] For instance, if I am sickened by coarse and simple food, it is the concupiscence of the flesh that troubles me, causing my food to be disagreeable to me. And the reason for my having to make an effort to dominate my disinclination is that I have not yet cast off fully the yoke of cupidity, for my discomfort is certainly not caused by the yoke of Christ.

If, on the other hand, I am consumed by a longing for rich banquets—and if in addition food that is poor or served late, or badly prepared and insufficient to my normal needs, fills me with disgust—the only reason for my vexation is that I am filled with the passion of greed instead of with the sweetness of charity. And if a monk demands of his superior as many dishes at meals as he sings nocturns in choir—and caps this with expecting the quality of his meals to go up in the same degree as the rank of feast being celebrated on that day, looking forward to rare dainties brought from afar—it is all because his greed outweighs his charity. For if any such question of food as we have discussed here should give rise to contention and grumbling and raised voices and disturb the peace of the monastery, it is only because worldly lusts have enslaved men's hearts, and so brought trouble and disagreement on them. Wars and quarrels arise among us, as Saint James explains, because our concupiscences are at war in our members.[5]

The necessity of penance

Now when I say that the body has to be weakened by
vigils, daily manual work and poor food, some people will,
I know, object that this not only implies a great deal of
effort, but it also means that charity itself will suffer. This,
they claim, is because labour and hard work take away
all the delight that the soul might inwardly experience in
the enjoyment of God's love. Such is the foolish opinion
of those who say that any trouble experienced by the body
must be bad for the soul. They assert that bodily suffering
is bound to diminish holiness, and in fact they seem to think
that the soul's enjoyment of God, even on this earth, must
somehow consist in the complete absence of pain for the
body. Since body and soul naturally cleave together, they
say, their sufferings must necessarily be communicated to
each other.[6] Thus the soul's peace must certainly be disturbed if the body is in any way afflicted! To their great
shame, they use the rules of Hippocrates for laying down
the law in respect of divine grace, so that when they claim
to investigate such matters with the help of doctors of
medicine instead of following the gospel precepts, they are
hopelessly misled. They pride themselves on their wisdom,
but it is an earthly wisdom, an animal cunning, a subtlety
worthy of the devil. Theirs is certainly not the wisdom that
comes down from above—modest, peace-loving wisdom.
Rather is it the wisdom of mere words which tries to do
away with the cross of Christ by means of bodily ease.

But the cross has nothing in common with delicate living
or soft habits, for it is itself the complete contradiction of
a comfortable way of life. The nails, the lance, the wounds—
all these have had their way with the flesh of Christ, and in
my opinion nothing that the flesh suffers can in any way do

43

harm to the spirit. Having the authority of the holy fathers behind me, I would uphold this truth against all comers. For if one bears the sufferings of the flesh with a right intention, and if one follows the example of the saints of the past without depending on one's own ideas—which means that one must have a true discretion that is neither half-hearted nor irrationally severe—then the soul's consolation will in no way be lessened. On the contrary, there will, without any doubt, be an increase of it. I would even go so far as to say that there is always a proportion between the two; in other words, where suffering abounds, consolation will abound equally. But this is not to deny that God, for some good reason, may give consolation more abundantly to someone who is not leading a particularly severe life, and that He may withdraw it from someone else whose life is extremely austere. However this does not make God any the less loving, kind or compassionate. Yet since whatever I may say on the matter will be of less authority than that of Christ Himself, let us see what our Lord says, and remember that to disagree with His words is heresy.

6

Teaching of Scripture on penance

I SUGGEST that we let the question be answered by one in whom Christ has very clearly spoken, namely Saint Paul, who suffered all tribulations—fears within and conflicts without[7]—and reduced his body to slavery. Never did he eat a mouthful of bread that he had not earned himself, and he worked with his hands for his own sustenance and that of those who were with him. He was Christ's most faithful witness, Christ's champion, bearing with hunger and thirst, cold and nakedness. He can show as no one else can whether weariness and suffering do away with spiritual consolation. We might well expect to find here a heart and mind so sorely tried that they had no room for tears or for any experience of the sweetness of divine grace. But what do we find in fact? We find him writing with tears to those who mourn, and weeping over the sinner who has not yet done penance for his sins. We see him rejoicing with those who rejoice, and sighing that he might be clothed with a new life from on high.

As for his spiritual delight, how can I even speak of that which he makes so clear when he says that by comparison with the joy he tastes in the love of God, all earthly advantages can only be considered as if they were dung.[8] And when he says how he longs to have done with this life and to be with Christ,[9] he can have been moved only by extreme delight to say such a thing. For him to have been able to say that he will glory only in the cross of the Lord Jesus Christ,[10] must have meant that he was on fire with the love of Christ. And this we can see again when he says: *If any man love not our Lord Jesus Christ, let him be anathema!*[11]

Let Saint Paul tell us whether or not he was left without consolation in his trials, and then we may have some guidance about what we may expect in our own tribulations. Let his words deal the death blow to any insidious suggestion that divine grace is likely to abound the more in a less strict form of living. Let him destroy the idea that one may be more holy in feasting and drunkenness than in the poverty and purity of the gospel, or in hunger, thirst, vigils, hard toil and tribulation, or in the mortification of self-will, or in the contempt of the world and the flesh. And if anyone still thinks that there is more consolation in the pleasures of the flesh than in its mortification, let him take to heart the words: *Blessed be the God and Father of our Lord Jesus Christ who comforts us in all our tribulations.*[12] That is to say, whether we suffer hunger, or are burdened with work, or

45

are wearied with lack of sleep, God is always to be blessed, for He gives us consolation always—even though we should be stoned, beaten or imprisoned.

The sufferings of Christ abound in us, Paul tells us, so that through Christ our consolation may also abound.[13] And as I said before, there is a proportion between suffering and consolation. Who, then, could be so stupid as to affirm that our share in Christ's sufferings is bad for our souls, with only the arguments of doctors of medicine for his authority? As our authority we may take the words of Saint Benedict in his *Rule for Monks*, where he says that we should persevere in the monastery until the end, sharing in Christ's sufferings, that is, in His passion, by means of the virtue of patience.[14] And this we are to do so that we may share His kingdom with Him in the life to come. Now this share in Christ's passion includes all our subjection to the discipline of the Rule—our abstinence, our vigils, our toil, the subjection of our own will to the will of others, and our putting obedience before all else. Moreover, all these bodily sufferings are necessary for us, since our outward nature falls away in time, while our inner nature is renewed. In this life we have to bear a few small trials which are nothing in comparison with the glory that is being stored up for us in heaven.

Give strong drink to them that are sad, and wine to them that are grieved in mind.[15] Solomon says this of the wine of consolation that rejoices the heart, and not of the ordinary wine on which men get drunk. And notice that it is kept for those who are sad and grieved in mind. *Let them drink and forget their want*, he adds, plainly implying that consolation comes as a reward, for it makes a man forget all his efforts and labour. When many cares filled his heart, the psalmist tells us,[16] God's comforting love made his soul rejoice. Therefore let no one be afraid of the rough way that leads to eternal life, or turn back through fear to the lax manner of life that he may have followed in time past. But, as Saint Benedict says, let him sustain all the difficulties, and neither faint nor look back, knowing that the more he bears with his difficulties for Christ's sake, the more his soul will rejoice with consolation.

7

Spiritual consolations

NOVICES have often asked me why it is that they tend to experience less spiritual consolation in the monastery than in the world. They recall how, in the past, they often felt great contrition of heart together with the sweetness of God's visitation, despite the fact that at the time they were living in luxury with more than enough to eat and drink, with more sleep than they needed, with tasteful clothes, no work, no observance of silence to get on their nerves. Why should it be, they have asked, that in the monastery they are dry, with no feeling of compunction, no consciousness of the love of God?

My answer has been to agree that it is fully possible for a man to experience contrition and the sweetness of God's visitation, though at the same time he is swallowed up in all the sins that go with the pleasures of the world. Such a man may often weep for his sins—indeed, it would be surprising if he did not—and not for his sins only but also for the love of Jesus. But this does not mean that we can emulate his sinful life just for the sake of enjoying the spiritual consolations that may incidentally attend it. For it must be observed that these spiritual visitations are not always an indication of sanctity. Sometimes they are designed to instill a longing for holiness, while at other times they are meant as helps for the continuance of a holy life.

47

In fact we can consider three kinds of heavenly visitation, the first awaking in us a desire for God, the second being our consolation on our way to God, and the third forming our reward. The first is for those who are still asleep in their sins, the second for those who are trudging along the road to heaven, and the third for those who long for paradise. It is as a favour that the first is given, either to attract those who are disinclined or to warn those who are negligent. But the second is a help and encouragement for those who have already made a beginning, while the third already welcomes those who have not far left to go. Thus we may say that the first is a goad, the second may be compared to a pilgrim's staff, while the third is a bed of rest and quiet.

Most of us have seen how the mercy of God will bring a negligent man back into the way of salvation by some word or example, or by some correction or even punishment. The inner compunction that either arouses fear in him or stimulates his love, draws him on to a better way of life. There are two reasons for this visitation of divine grace: it can be meant either as a warning to those who live evil lives, or as an encouragement to those who do well.

8

Compunction in saints and sinners

IT is not at all surprising that the same grace should be given alike to the good and the bad, since the better gifts, as Saint Paul calls them,[17] are all granted to the good and bad alike— for instance the gifts of knowledge, prophecy and tongues, and the grace of miracles. Proof of this may be found in Saul who was a prophet, or in Judas who was an apostle. And Our Lord tells us how on judgement day many will ask Him if it was not in His name that they cast out devils and worked miracles, and He will answer that He never knew them.[18]

From the Old Testament we know that Balaam experienced compunction, for he asked God to let him die, and to let his end be the end of a just man.[19] Yet although he deplored his own wickedness, his sorrow did no good to his soul, since we find him afterwards teaching Balac to give scandal to others by fornication, drunkenness and eating food sacrificed to idols. And we also read how often the children of Israel wept before God when Moses upbraided them in the desert,[20] always returning afterwards to their evil ways. And when led into the Promised Land,[21] even when they had lifted up their voices with grief at the place of weeping, they did evil again in the sight of God. Then in the New Testament we read that Judas himself knew compunction when he confessed that he had sinned in betraying the blood of a just man.[22]

But compunction means nothing if we go back to our evil ways after having been contrite, for *he that washes himself after touching the dead, if he touches him again, what does his washing avail?*[23] To wash ourselves after touching the dead can mean, for us, that we bury the evil of our past lives and weep for sorrow at what is over and done. But having buried the past, we must amend our lives, otherwise we have wept in vain. Now for those whom God loves, all things work together for good,[24] and so compunction for them is not meant as a warning but as an encouragement to do better. And after this heavenly visitation they never let themselves fall back into dissolute ways. Instead, the more they taste and enjoy the sweetness of God coming into their souls, the stronger and more zealous they are to do better in the future.

The purpose of consolation

ANYONE who throws off spiritual indifference and takes on sweat and labour for the love of Christ is likely to receive that wonderful kind of compunction which heals the sick in soul, strengthens the weak and comforts the despairing. It comes as a consolation to those who mourn, a rest for those who labour, a protection for those who are tempted, and a refreshment for those who are trudging along the way to God. But it is a consolation that can be easily taken away if we are discouraged by the first trials that come to meet us, if we fall back into the ways of negligence, or if we take too easily to the consolations of worldly society or to the liberties of our own free will. Of these vain consolations the psalmist has said that his soul refused to find comfort in them,[25] yet, for all that, he was not left without consolation, since he says that he remembered God, and this filled his soul with delight. Like the first, this visitation also has two reasons: to those who are being tempted it may be given to save them from succumbing, and it may also be given to those who are about to be tempted that they may be the better able to bear with the temptation when it comes.

But whether God's grace comes to sustain the soul or to fortify it, in neither case can it be taken as a sign of holiness. For grace can come to sustain even the soul of a man who has been leading a life of sin, and although it can make ready the way for grace, it is in no wise an indication that the soul is already holy. First the soul must be born into grace, and then it must be nourished on grace. And during this time of nourishment the soul may often be blessed with feelings of compunction and with spiritual consolations. But these are meant to carry the soul on to that stage at which, being strong against evil, it will receive grace as its reward for having overcome evil.

God's work in the soul

In the soul's first state, then, it is roused, in the second it is purified, and in the third it enjoys its Sabbath rest. And God shows first His mercy, then His kindness, and finally His justice, with mercy seeking that which was lost, with kindness helping the soul in its struggle against evil, and with justice finally giving the victor his crown. And what, indeed, could be a greater sign of divine clemency than that the pure sweetness, joy and serenity of God should come down to the soul that is still foul with sin? It is firstly the fear of God that knocks on the door of the soul, but once this is done every obstacle is overcome by divine grace, whose sweetness comes like a kiss to the lips of the soul, however impure they may have become through vicious habit. This coaxes the soul to turn away from evil, it draws us onwards when we hesitate, and brings back life and hope when these are waning.

O sweet Lord, what shall I give Thee back for all Thou hast given me? How sweet and gentle is Thy spirit in every way! For great is Thy mercy towards me, since Thou hast stretched out Thy hand from above to free me from the power of my enemies and from the danger of drowning in the flood. And Thou hast snatched my soul from the depths of hell from the very moment when I first tasted Thy sweetness there, hearing Thy voice as if it came from afar.

'How much longer will you remain in that filth, unworthy and unclean soul?' the Creator might ask. 'How long will you go on finding your delight in what is disgusting? Consider instead the sweetness that is Mine to give you, for what could be more delightful and pleasing in every way? Are you to despair because of the great

number of your evil days? Shall I cast off the one who
comes thus to Me when I must punish him who runs away?
No indeed, I embrace and draw to Me the face that would
turn from me, so it is not likely that I would repulse anyone
who comes to take refuge in My mercy.'

Such inspirations as these, sent from God, are His voice.
And to the soul that has known despair, hope can come from
nowhere but from God, who cares for us in our weakness
and restores us to health.

Then we come to the second state of which we have
spoken, in which God's kindness goes to work in a wonderful manner in the souls and lives of men, helping them to
make progress through temptations, and strengthening
them by their experience of frailty. Of its nature every soul
runs away from what is painful and laborious, but now
there is such abounding consolation, even in temptation,
that God's grace enables us to overcome. Thus the soul is
not only able to bear with temptation; now it even welcomes it, as the psalmist did when he said: *Prove me, O Lord,
and try me . . . prove me, O God, and know my heart.*[26]

In this state the soul gradually becomes accustomed to so
much consolation that it is eventually drawn into the further
phase which we have already mentioned, in which it experiences some foretaste of the future reward, moving, as it
were, into the house of God's holiness, into His very
dwelling place. There the soul is carried up to the contemplation and enjoyment of God, and it says, as David did:
*This is my rest for ever and ever. Here will I dwell for I have
chosen it.*[27] Notice that in the second stage there was no
preceding merit on our part, for the mercy of God did
everything. But in the third state in which God rewards
and crowns His own gifts in our souls, He has considered
these as our merits none the less, and so in rewarding them
His mercy and justice work together.

The fruits of God's visitations

I WOULD like to point out here that in the first state—I mean the first of God's visitations to the soul—the sweetness of consolation is often not without some experience of the fear of God. In the second state there is quite often some little goad of this same fear, but the emphasis is none the less on the enjoyment of His love. But in the third state, charity now being perfect, there is no place at all for fear. The beginning of wisdom is the fear of the Lord, we read,[28] and its consummation is certainly God's love, for love must leave fear behind. Yet it cannot be left behind unless it turns into love. The soul that knows fear also knows sadness, pain, despair perhaps, and tedium, but as soon as the slightest taste of God's love or the slightest beam of His light come into the soul, all these feelings disappear. The heart unburdens and expands, and the soul rejoices and delights in God so that it seems to fly up to heaven on wings. For fear casts out any lukewarmness that may remain in the soul after its conversion; but it is a fear tempered by a taste of the divine love. In fact, fear is given to us only to prevent us taking our rest in things that are unworthy. But the experience of God's love in the soul enables us to overcome the discouragement that great labour may engender. Thus fear and love alternate in the soul, teaching us necessary lessons in this life until such time as the whole soul is thoroughly penetrated by love and it longs for the embrace of Christ. For there comes a time when we grow tired of waiting, and we yearn to be dissolved in Christ and made one with Him.

Thus we can count three degrees in this process, which are three divine visitations. Firstly there is the compunction that makes us conscious of sin. On this first visitation no one can pride himself, since it is designed to rouse us from evil ways, or at least from our indifference. Likewise the second visitation is something on which we cannot compliment ourselves, since it is meant to give us strength when we are weak and when we tend to fall away. Only in the third, then, can we glory, although here we glory in the Lord, and thus only in this visitation can we find a sure sign of holiness.

12

God's consolation as the soul's strength

WE may sum up, therefore, by saying that the fruit of the first visitation is our conversion to God, while the second visitation means the mortification of all our passions and of our self-will, the final reward being perfect happiness. After the first compunction surely enough there comes the trial of temptations, which is just as it should be, for otherwise the soul would have nothing wherewith to merit the joys of the third visitation. Obviously it is highly unlikely that the sweet enjoyment of God's love should be bestowed without trials and temptations either foregoing or accompanying it or immediately following. Here there is no question of consolation coming as a reward, but simply as a support for us in weakness when we would otherwise fall.

Those who are discouraged by temptation and the need to make great efforts, are like the disciples who found our Lord's words hard.[29] They are scandalized, and will not take their share in the body and blood of the Lord, by which I mean that they will not share in His passion. They are no longer wholeheartedly in love with the kingdom of God, and they look back with yearning to the consolations of this world. Thus they cut themselves off from God's consolation, and in their wretchedness they will never come to the blessing of His final visitation, nor will they find the exercise of virtue anything but a burden. The only thing that we can say for them is that at least they do not go back to their former way of life, since their conscience is against doing so. But they could only be justified in pleading that consolation had deserted them, if they had indeed totally given up the past, were truly mortifying their wills, and were not preferring the futile consolations of the world to those of God.

But there are some who, as soon as they realize that their new way of life is hard and wearisome, lose themselves in a world of wishful thinking, looking forward to the time when they will be in a position to command rather than to obey, and presuming already on liberties that are not theirs to take. And so instead of waiting for the words, *Friend, go up higher*,[30] they put themselves forward and seek the first place, looking for honour and recognition, hoping that everyone may look up to them, and putting on superior airs—all this when they have not yet learned how to humble themselves and to follow a master's leading. Yet while all this is going on, they expect still to receive divine consolations in their souls. They think of nothing but worldly consolation, and yet they imagine that they are still fit subjects for the love of Jesus! If, however, it should happen that they do receive some little consolation from God, it is certainly not as a reward for their holiness, nor is it as a solace for their labours. Rather it is offered as an incentive to them, because they are still lazy about their salvation after having received the grace of conversion.

13

The measure of holiness

Now it is quite easy to ascertain for yourself why you receive the favours of God's love, not by following your own conjectures, but simply by observing the rules and conditions that we find throughout Holy Scripture. You remember, for instance, how our Lord warns us not to let our hearts become gross and heavy with eating and drinking and the cares of this world.[31] Neither must we be angry with our fellow men, lest we be guilty of the judgement; nor must we call them fools, lest we suffer for it in hell fire.[32] He also tells us that whoever has an ambition to be in authority must make himself the servant of all,[33] doing to others what he would wish them to do to him,[34] until one day he will have to give an account of every idle word he ever spoke.[35]

Then Saint Paul reminds us that we must put on the Lord Jesus Christ, and not give in to the desires of the flesh,[36] for no one who fights for God gets involved in the world's business.[37] He appeals to us to follow Christ's example of holiness more closely, and to run our own lives by working with our hands calmly and quietly, being fair to those who are in need and coveting nothing that belongs to others.[38] And he goes on to say that if anyone is unwilling to work, he has no right to his food.[39]

Then there is Saint James who tells us to have a true faith in Jesus Christ without any human respect to influence us in our showing of it.[40] Neither must we be contentious, for this leads to inconstancy and all sorts of bad deeds,[41] and the man who is a friend to this world cannot be a friend of God.[42]

Consider also the words of Saint Peter, the prince of the apostles, who begs us to abstain, like strangers and pilgrims, from fleshly desires.[43] We are to drop all malice, guile, insincerity, envy and detraction,[44] for when we speak we must speak the words of God.[45] And he offers a special word for pastors of souls, when he tells them not to be lovers of money or of authority, but to look after those committed to them.[46] And if we are young we are to be obedient to our elders, but we have all to be humble, one to another.[47] At all times sobriety and watchfulness are to be our characteristics.[48]

When we come to the exhortations of Saint John, the beloved disciple, we find first that whoever says he knows God and yet does not keep God's commandments, is a liar.[49] Do not love the world, he goes on to tell us, or the things that are in it. And he brands with the name of murderers those who hate their brethren.[50] Saint Jude in his turn begs us not to be murmurers, full of complaints, and living a life dedicated to the fulfilment of our own desires.[51] We must hate, he says, the spotted garment which is carnal.[52]

All these passages are the mirror in which you can catch the reflection of your own soul. There you will see if you are given to feasting and drinking, to the world's business and the desires of the flesh; whether you are querulous and contentious, whether you idle your days away in things that are useless; if you are given to backbiting, or are frivolous and unstable; if you are not an honest worker, but live sumptuously on the sweat of poor men's ill paid labour. You can soon see if you are an angry man, an impatient or envious man; whether you are an obedient monk or disobedient. You may be one of those who exercise their stomach muscles more than their brains. You may find that you are given to trespassing outside the limitations that your monastic profession lays down for you. And if you find that you are guilty of any such fault, do not, I beg you, think yourself a saint because you can weep tenderly during your devotions. Your tears may be simply the result of over-eating! And if, when you examine your soul in the mirror of Holy Scripture, you are stricken with fear and the love of God, then be careful not to abuse God's goodness by continuing as you have done in the past, lest your last state be worse than your first—a thing which, unfortunately, we see around us all too often every day.

14

The path of perseverance

IF, then, when you have given up the fleshpots of Egypt, the cares of this world and its striving and quarrelling, in exchange for the poverty of Christ and a life of obedience, do not be surprised if you do not immediately receive God's manna from heaven. You have crossed the Red Sea like a true Israelite; you have chosen solitude and silence, a life of brotherly love and voluntary poverty; you have escaped, in fact, from the tumult of this world. Do not, therefore, murmur against God if you do not yet experience the sweetness of His love. Do not wonder if indeed God is still with you, for Christ has said that if anyone loves God, he will keep God's commandments and God will love him, coming to him and living in his soul.[53] Do not allow into your mind any blasphemous thought that might suggest to you that the service of God is all in vain and that there is no reward for those who keep His commandments.[54]

You may even be tempted to feel, as the psalmist felt, that you have justified your heart in vain, that you have washed your hands among the innocent,[55] and that you have been punished for doing so, whereas sinners are seen to abound in wealth, and even—it might seem to you—in spiritual consolation. And if, as you possibly suspect, there is more consolation from God in a life of luxury, then you might be tempted to think it better to eat and drink and enjoy the good things of this world rather than those of the life to come. Yet you need not be surprised that you do not immediately receive heavenly consolation, when you remember Saint Paul's reminder that we cannot enter into the kingdom of God without suffering many tribulations in this life.[56] These trials must not make us waver, he tells us, since they are our appointed lot.[57]

The children of Israel were often roused in Egypt by the sight of wonderful miracles performed on their behalf, and there too they ate of the Paschal Lamb; but after they had crossed the Red Sea they were not *immediately* given manna from heaven to eat. Far from it, they were led first to the bitter waters of Mara and tempted there. Only after that, when they were led by the twelve springs into the secret place of the desert, were they filled with the bread from heaven.[58]

And so you too, who have left Egypt behind you and gone dryshod through the Red Sea, will first be led to the bitter waters, where labour and weariness will cast you down, and there you will find how true it is that the way of life is a narrow way.[59] God will tempt you indeed, but you must be one of those of whom Christ can say: *You are they who have continued with Me in my temptation.*[60] Then you will go on to the twelve fountains which are the teachings of the twelve apostles, which you will carefully ponder in Holy Scripture. The Scriptures will carry you out of this world, God's words giving you, as it were, the wings of a dove that will bear you to the silent places of the Spirit. But there you must remember, if God should send you the manna of His consolation from heaven, that it is not yours to dispose of, collect or keep as you wish. For the children of Israel discovered, if they went to seek the manna on a Sabbath day, that there was none to be found. And if they gathered more than the quantity that

God commanded, they would find on the morrow that it had already corrupted.[61]

But when God does console you with His love, you must not think that all your labours are at an end. There must still be prayer to fight temptation and the lusts of your fallen nature. For only after much trouble and striving may the soul be rewarded by the most wonderful of all God's visitations, and set so completely on fire by charity that all lusts are burned away. Then at last there is rest in the contemplation of God, in His perfect peace, and in the fullness of His wisdom. And then you will know indeed how light the Lord's burden is, and how gentle His yoke.[62]

15

Conversation with a novice

PERHAPS in conclusion I cannot do better than to give you the example of a novice I used to have, who came to me one day and asked me why it was that he had received in his previous worldly condition much more spiritual consolation—both of compunction and of the extreme feeling of God's love—than he did in the monastery. The question, as you see, is exactly the one we have been discussing in these chapters.

I answered him by asking him a question, namely did he think that the life he had led in the world was holier and more acceptable to God than the way of life he followed in the monastery? To this he answered that this was far from the case, and if, in those days, he had done any of the things he was now doing in the monastic life, all his old friends would immediately have thought him a saint. So I then asked him if, in those days, he had ever considered how Saint Paul tells us that we must go through many tribulations to get to the kingdom of God. And I asked him if it had ever occurred to him that not even a just man may lift up his head, since he is filled with affliction and misery.[63] He admitted that he had never reflected on any such ideas, but had rather been conscious of loving Christ very deeply.

And therefore I asked him if, this being so, he suffered as much for Christ's sake in those days as he did now as a novice in religion. To this he replied that in those days he would not have tolerated for a single hour the mortifications that he bore daily in the monastic life. 'I would never, for instance, have spent a whole day in absolute silence', he said. 'Far from it, I used to spend my whole life just chattering about this and that. I did weep real tears when I thought of how much I loved Christ, but that didn't stop me from going straight back to my usual amusements, the company of friends and relatives, eating too much, drinking too much, sleeping late into the day, giving way to every feeling of anger or discontent, fighting, coveting other people's property, and indulging my own will in every way.'

Here I asked him to describe by contrast the life he lived as a novice. He smiled and replied: 'That's easy enough! Just look at me! My clothes, for instance—they are so rough. The food I eat is, by comparison with what I used to eat, unbearably coarse, and all I have to drink now is water. As for sleep, I spend as much time nodding into my books as I do on my bed! And when I go to bed I am utterly worn out, but just at the very moment when sleep is pleasantest and I feel I could go on sleeping for hours, the bell rings for matins. And there is hardly any need to add how we really do work for our bread in the sweat of our brow. I am allowed to speak with three people only— and even that is very seldom. We certainly mortify our members in our way of life.[64] We are in fact just like the psalmist's beasts of burden,[65] going wherever we are sent without a murmur, carrying on our backs whatever is put on them. There is no place for self-will and no time for idleness. But at the same time you cannot help realizing that there are so many good things to make up for what is hard. We never quarrel, for instance. We are never angry with one another, never have the poor coming to complain that we are defrauding them of their rights. We never get involved in litigation of any sort, and there is peace everywhere here, silence and calm. We are completely free from the tumult of the world. There is such unity among the brethren, so much concord, that everything belongs to everyone. And what I love above everything else is that there is no consideration of persons for the rank they held in the world, for birth makes no difference here. We are only treated differently according to our needs—if we are ill, for instance, or not very strong. The fruits of our common work are divided among all, with nothing extra for favourites, but only for those in need. It is absolutely marvellous to me that in this monastery three hundred men can obey the commands of one superior, and do everything he says as if they had all agreed among themselves on this one thing, or as if they had heard the voice of God telling them to do it. In fact I seem to find here every perfection that the gospel precepts contain, and everything I read in the teaching of the fathers and of the monks of old.'

'Since you are a novice', I said, 'I can put all this enthusiasm down to fervour, and not to self-satisfaction! But you must be careful to remember that there is no perfection in this life that may not be cleverly aped by people who are insincere. And I don't want you to be put off by them, when you discover frauds in the religious life, as you certainly will. But tell me, now that you have described the monastic life in such detail, is it to be compared with those precious tears which you wept in the world?'

'Heaven forbid', he replied, 'that my conscience should be calmed by a few tears, or that tears alone should take away the fear of the last judgement! Only now, in this monastery, am I at peace in my soul, and so can look forward calmly to the time when God will take me. Of course, you will probably say that this is only weakness on my part, and that I am weary of life because the monastic routine is sometimes so wearisome. But the only reason why I could depart a life of mortification is that God is merciful, and I know it. That is why it is so very odd that I seemed to love God more in those days, when in fact I was much less sure of His mercy.'

'Well, you can put it this way', I said. 'Supposing you had two servants, and one of them was very obedient—and not only obedient, but let us say he would put up with a lot of trouble on your account—while the other one was so disobedient that he transgressed your commands every day, and would certainly never dream of putting himself to any trouble or inconvenience to please you. Now if both of these servants said that they loved you, which one would you be more inclined to believe?'

'I would say that the one was as much to be rewarded as the other was to be punished', the novice replied.

'In that case, you can judge yourself in the same way', I said.

We went on discussing the question in this same vein, until he asked me if it were better to consider completely worthless all the tender feelings of love he used to experience in the world, all the tears he shed for the love of Christ. And therefore I felt it necessary to make it very plain that this was far from being the case. I explained that in fact these tears and feelings were, in their way, extremely useful. 'But you must remember', I said, 'not to judge your love for God by these passing feelings and emotions, since we may even be moved to tears by a very good performance on a stage.'

'How true', he answered quickly. 'That is exactly what

63

used to happen to me when I heard them telling the story of King Arthur. And now I think of it, I sometimes feel quite proud of myself when I am moved to tears by the story of our Lord's sufferings in the gospel or in a good sermon. But I can see now how stupid it is if I give way to vainglory for the sake of a passing emotion, just as I used to when I listened to romances. But you were saying, if I remember, that feelings and tears could be useful in some way. In what way do you mean?'

'I mean that these things will give you some knowledge of the truth, so that you may come to know yourself and may learn not to spare your own faults. Look how often, even against their own conscience, people put forward clever and deceptive arguments which give them an excuse for hiding their own faults even from themselves. Like the church of Laodicea in Saint John's revelation, they think that now that they have come into their own, they are rich and want for nothing,[66] when in fact they are wretched, miserable, poor, blind and naked. It would be far better for them to say with the psalmist: *Have mercy on me, O Lord, for I am weak.*[67] Such feelings and tears will, in fact, show you not that you are wonderfully holy, but that you are weak and needy.'

16

The will as love

OUR love of God, then, must not be gauged by the passing feelings we experience that are not controlled by the will, but rather we must judge them by the enduring quality of the will itself. For loving God means that we join our will to God's will. It means that our will consents to whatever the will of God commands. It means that we have only one

64

reason for wishing anything, and the reason is that we know that God wills it.

The will, after all, is nothing if not love, so that when we speak of the will as being good or bad, we are thinking in terms of good love or bad love. God's will is God's love, and His will and His love are none other than the Holy Spirit, by whom charity is poured forth in our hearts. And this pouring out of love is simply the joining together of God's will with our own. As Saint Paul says,[68] whoever cleaves to God becomes one spirit with Him. For the Holy Spirit, who is the will and the love of God, so floods our human wills that He transforms them into Himself, drawing them up to God and away from all that is beneath us. Thus the human will is made so to cleave to God that it becomes one spirit with the Holy Spirit, who is God.

The quality of our will can be judged by two things, namely by the way we bear with whatever God sends us in the way of sufferings, and by the way we fulfil His commands. We are judged, in other words, by what we do for God and by what we patiently allow Him to do to us. As Saint Gregory tells us,[69] no one need account himself anything unless his works reflect something of the love of God. And in the same way our Lord tells us that the man who loves Him is the man who keeps the commandments which he has from Him.[70]

The visitations of God's grace that come to us in the form of feelings and emotions, are for God to bestow when and where and to whom He wills. It is not for us to seek them, or even to ask for them, and if God should suddenly remove them from us, our wills must be in agreement with His. For the man who loves God is the man who bears patiently with all that God does to him, and who is zealous in carrying out God's precepts. If love were to be judged by feeling, this would mean that we only love God and our fellow men when we feel love towards God and towards our brethren.

And so we would have to conclude that a continuous and persistent love was impossible, and that we could love only on certain privileged occasions.

If, say, a just man should wish the salvation of someone and God did not wish it, we could not say that this man's will was not in accord with God's will. God wants all men to be saved, and His will works through the will of men. In this case, God would be making our just man form precisely the right desire of another's salvation.

This love has its beginners, its proficients, and its adepts. Now, merely to feel love for God is not the same as loving God, but it is at least a beginning of love, and it forms a strong attraction to a fuller love of God. It is one thing to strive after a sweet feeling of the love of God, and another to experience the feeling of God's love when one is not looking for it. In the one case we love without tasting, and in the other we taste without loving. In other words, the man who loves God is the man who keeps His commandments and leads a good life; and so the man who feels the love of God in his soul daily without laying down his own will to God's commands, does not yet love God.

17

The various fruits of compunction

THIS feeling of the love of God is a great encouragement to good works for those who have been diffident about serving God. But for those whose lives are already dedicated to doing good, the sweetness of love comes as a necessary consolation when they tend to tire. And for those who have reached the heights of Christian perfection, the experience of love is a refreshment that cannot be taken away from them. Thus God, who is wonderfully merciful to us all, effects our salvation in these various ways. He draws us to Himself with the delights of love, He warns us with His justice, and He enlightens us with wisdom. It is as if you were to try to convince someone who had never tasted it, that honey is the sweetest thing in the world. No one could be convinced by words alone. But as soon as God gives us a taste of even one drop of His sweet love, that taste creates such an appetite in our souls that we will do anything to have more of it. And whenever the labour involved in achieving our desire becomes too much, a little drop of the sweetness of love will restore our strength. Our merciful Saviour draws us to His salvation by the experience of His love, and leads us away from the temptations of the flesh; and this is more than reason or the fear of hell can do when temptation is very strong. He puts on us the yoke of His service, and we become so much attached to Him that in the end we are made His simply by the delight of loving Him, for every man is drawn by what delights him.[71]

But whoever desires to serve God must bear in mind the call of the book of Ecclesiasticus to be strong and to prepare his soul for temptation.[72] Whenever temptation threatens to become too much and we start to fall and despair, if only a drop of the love of God touches our lips, we are wonderfully refreshed, and we can go back to the struggle stronger than before. We find ourselves more patient, more brave, more able to overcome temptation and to shun it. Afterwards it may well happen that, despite the experience of love that God has bestowed on us, we go back to our stupid and light-minded habits, but when we do so we are overcome by a very salutary sense of shame. This is when a man will conceive the ambition to take up a stricter way of life, so that, even though his will should yearn for what is base and frivolous, he is fortunately no longer in a position to indulge his desires.

67

More advice to a novice

I WAS speaking in this vein to the novice mentioned a few chapters ago, and I asked him if he did not see that his fervent conversion and his present austere mode of living were the fruit of his original contrition. 'These are the outcome of your tears', I told him. 'God used your sorrow to work out your salvation. Therefore is it surprising that when your deep feeling of contrition has done its work, it should disappear? The work you have now in hand is that of suffering all for Christ's sake, to exercise the virtue of patience, to overcome the overbearing flesh with vigils and fasts, to bear temptations without giving in to them, and to call away your soul from everything that savours of the world. With the virtue of obedience you must mortify your will. And whenever you are wearied by all the labours of your present state of life, you must go to Jesus by means of sincere prayer to draw, as it were, the milk of consolation from the breast of Him who is a mother to you. God indeed is blessed who comforts us in every tribulation.[73] For Christ's sufferings abound now in us, but only so that our consolations may abound the more. In the beginning of your conversion you were given the sweet feeling of God's love in order to draw you away from evil. And after that you will find that consolation comes to refresh you on your way, so that you may not be overcome by this hard life. Finally, when you have mastered the many trials and difficulties that give you trouble at the moment, you will find that great abundance of sweetness which is laid up for those that fear the Lord.'[74]

At this my young novice said, with tears in his eyes, that he hoped to God that it would all come to pass as I had said, for he already knew the sweetness of God's love as it comes at the beginning of the soul's conversion. Also he was beginning to realize how consolation comes during the soul's trials in order to give it comfort on the way. 'And I trust', he added, 'that I shall one day also experience the great abundance of God's sweetness.'

'At least you see', I answered, 'how differently things in fact turn out from the way you had visualized them.'

'How do you mean?' he asked.

'You have discovered', I replied, 'that you love God much less than you thought you did. I mean that it is precisely when you thought that you loved God most that you find you loved Him less. The more negligent we are of our salvation and the more our souls are weak, the more imperfect our love is, don't you agree? And now that you know yourself a little better, you discover that God sends His consolations in the first place to show us the error of our ways; and when we have accepted the fact that we are at fault, and amend our lives, consolation helps us not to be overcome by the weariness of that amendment. But in neither case is love perfect.'

'Yes, they are sadly mistaken', he agreed with a sigh, 'who part with their salvation so easily by refusing to give up things that are bad. If they could only experience a little of the love you have been speaking about, not only would they be offered forgiveness for their past sins, but they would also be given more of the same delight in God's love. Yet often the encouragement that God gives us to abandon our evil lives profits us nothing. It makes us feel a little holier, perhaps, but we go back to our bad ways none the less, and even a little more determinedly than before. Then although we have been given by God a spirit of remorse, our eyes still do not see, nor do our ears hear.[75] There is, I suppose, a sort of remorse that makes us blind, and deaf as well, since we imagine that tears alone are enough to wash away our sins, when in fact we must prove our sorrow by works of penance.'

'Tears are something very precious to God', I answered, 'and they are sufficient sacrifice to atone for all our past sins, but only if we are truly penitent and confess our sins, and with a contrite spirit fly to Jesus and do all that we can to make amends. For how can there be true penance if we return to our evil ways? And therefore you, who are a novice, must work out your salvation with labour and care, with mortification of the flesh, with vigils and manual work, with poor food and rough clothes, with silence and recollection. These will make an acceptable sacrifice of your whole being—both the inner and the outward man—and tears will enkindle the flame of charity that it sends up to God. But even if you have no tears it is sufficient to embrace the poverty of a perfect Christian life, and to live by the truth of the gospel. This is far better than to pour out tears every day while disobeying God's commandments. For if we consistently do evil, all our tears will avail us nothing. And even if our tears had the power to raise the dead, to cast out devils and to give sight to the blind, our Lord would still say at the last day, *Depart from me.*'[76]

19

Zeal in progressing

ALL these considerations are not without a certain relevance, since, if we bear them carefully in mind, we shall see quite easily how a novice in his fervour may be lifted up by the lightness of heart brought by God's grace, and at the same time be burdened down by the weight of his natural desires for earthly things. The more deeply rooted in his soul these desires are, the harder it will be to turn away from them and to raise the mind to God.

70

Here we may take as our example the lazy man who has a field with a few weeds in it, and the industrious man whose whole field is overgrown with weeds. It is the latter, not the former, who will have his field cleared more quickly. Likewise, if a novice has a few bad habits and is lazy about eradicating them, he will not make as much progress as the one who has many bad habits but is more industrious about reforming his life. The former gives up the world, but is slow and tepid and altogether less diligent about the purification of his soul, although in the world he may not have been considered at all a bad man. He will come to the state of perfect peace of soul and to true freedom in the love of God later than the man who is full of zeal in rooting out the evil from his soul by taking up the tools of the spiritual craft. For only where there is fervour and diligence and the virtue of discretion, can the evil yoke of lusts and passions be thrown off, and the gentle yoke and light burden of the Lord be put on in its place.

20

The curbing of the flesh

WHOEVER finds all this out for himself will agree that, although the curbing of the flesh is a burdensome thing, none the less there is great delight and no labour at all when the soul is filled with the sweetness of purity. There is a sense of victory when we are no longer slaves to our stomachs. We can then say with Saint Paul that we have learned to be content with the circumstances in which we find ourselves, for we have learned like him what it is to be brought low, and what it is to have plenty of what we need. Like him also we shall have learned to go hungry or to be well fed, to live in plenty or to live in want.[77] For when the lusts of the flesh are quietened, or rather absorbed by the love of God, there is nothing hard in a life of virtue, because the soul has nothing to disturb it any more that cannot be dissolved in love.

To control the pleasures of the eyes and ears must necessitate a certain amount of effort on the part of those who have not wholly accepted the yoke of Christ. For where bad habits have been already formed, the Lord's yoke is not found to be a light burden. On the contrary, it may seem very hard indeed, since it implies the contempt of all pleasures. But in fact the liberty which is bestowed on those who know how to despise pleasures, is quite as great as the delights that these vanities afford to those who still enjoy them.

I shall not, however, say anything here about the pleasures of the sense of smell, because, although there are plenty of people who do abuse this sense, monks are unlikely to find much trouble in losing the taste for sweet scents and smells that are pleasant.

21

The pleasures of hearing

SINCE we are not speaking here of those who are openly given to bad ways, I shall consider those who use religion as a pretext for justifying the pleasures which our ears may enjoy. Under the old dispensation musical instruments were allowed, since they were figures of the truth yet to come. But now that the Church has outgrown the stage of types and figures, what are we doing, I often wonder, with the thunder of organ music, the clash of cymbals, and elaborate part-settings for different voices? We hear monks doing all sorts of ridiculous things with their voices, plaguing us with womanish falsettos, spavined bleating and tremolos. I myself have seen monks with open mouths, not so much singing, as doing ludicrous feats of breathing, so that they looked as if they were in their last agony or lost in rapture. I have even seen them waving their arms about, beating time to the music, and contorting their bodies in all directions. And they honestly do this in the name of religion, for they think that they are giving God a greater honour than if they sang without all this fuss. The simple folk who hear them may well be impressed by the organ music, but they cannot help laughing as they see such a ridiculous show going on in the choir. They are in fact more likely to think that they are watching a stage play than praying in church. There is no awe here before the dread majesty of God, and no respect for the holy table at which Christ is lapped in linen and His most precious blood poured out, where heaven opens and angels throng about us, bringing earth and heaven together. The practices that the holy fathers of old ordered and laid down for their simple people, that they might be moved to devotion and the love of God, have become nothing but an excuse for frivolous pleasure, and the mere sound of singing is preferred to the meaning of the words that are sung.

Sense and sound together are meant to stir us to devotion, and therefore the sound of our music must be sober and moderate. It must keep within its appointed bounds and not trespass on the words, so that our minds are distracted from their meaning. Saint Augustine admits that our souls may well be drawn to devotion through hearing songs sung, but he insists that if we find more joy in the sound than in the sense of what is sung, we are none the better off for it.[78] And again he says that if he felt he was getting more pleasure from the tune than from the words, he would feel that he sinned gravely, and would rather not hear the singers at all.

If anyone who has turned his back on the foolish vanities of which we are speaking, should be tempted to return to them, and should prefer these barbarous contortions and technician's refinements to the simple and true mode of singing laid down by Augustine, Ambrose and Gregory, it is easy enough to see how the conflict between two such contrary tastes comes about. It is worldly concupiscence—not the yoke of charity—that irks him.

22

The wandering of the eyes

IT is now time to say something about the lust of the eyes, which the holy fathers call curiosity or inquisitiveness, for it is not merely an external vice. It has its inner aspect too. As regards the external aspect, to start with, this covers the pleasures of those superficial attractions that the eyes delight in—the shape of things, their colour, the delicacy of their workmanship—in painting, sculpture, wrought vessels, clothes and shoes, and in all that is over and above basic necessity. The lover of this world is drawn into fleshly pleasure by such delights of the eyes.

When we are attracted to the outward show of things that are made with men's hands, we are leaving behind our Maker and bringing to nought the souls which are of His making. Thus there is no place at all in monasteries for the sculpture and painting that you find in other places—pictures and carvings, for instances, of cranes and hares, of harts and does, ravens and magpies. These are not the embellishments that Antony and Macarius sought in their desert hermitages; they are simply the ornaments of silly women. They are absolutely irreconcilable with monastic poverty; they are food for wandering eyes. And for the man who has bent his back to the yoke of divine love and found Jesus' company within his own soul, what use is there

74

for all the external pomps and shows that others love? Having once accepted the limitations of a life of bare necessity, he takes up with others of like mind, and shuns any sort of habitation that is too large or extravagantly vaulted—a wicked waste of space and materials. He is happy enough to say his prayers in a little chapel of rough, unpolished stone, where there is nothing carved or painted to distract the eye; no fine hangings, no marble pavements, no murals that depict ancient history or even scenes from Holy Scripture; no blaze of candles, no glittering of golden vessels. All such things will seem to have become loathsome to him; and to be in a place where such things are, will make him feel like one expelled from paradise and imprisoned in a dungeon of filth and squalor. He sees things as Saint Paul saw them, when he said that we look not at the things which are seen but at those which are not seen. For the things which are seen are temporal, but those which are not seen are eternal.[79]

This is the way that we learn to be meek and humble of heart, to find the hidden sweetness that is signified in the words, *All the glory of the king's daughter is within.*[80] All of us should examine our own lives, and so know what we are without having to judge ourselves by comparison with others.[81] And if in this way we are not to glory in other men, how much less can we have glory in objects that are dumb and senseless like gold and stone?

As to curiosity in its inward aspect, here we have to consider three things. Firstly there is the delight that men take in useless or even dangerous knowledge. Then there is the pleasure that we may be tempted to find in other people's lives, not for the sake of imitating their virtues but for criticizing their faults or envying them their worldly goods, or simply for the sake of satisfying idle curiosity. And lastly there is what we might call a general disturbance and preoccupation with the things of the world that results from all this. No little vexation of spirit is caused both to those who are thus immoderately occupied in vanities, and to those who would try to dissuade them from it. Often we meet with people who have given their minds to the empty philosophy of this world, and who are in the habit of reading the gospels in the same way that they read Virgil, studying Horace along with the prophets, and Cicero as if he were no different from Saint Paul. Such people are likely to acquire a taste for versifying, making up love songs and invectives—all of which things are, of course, forbidden by the Rule because they are the happy hunting ground for all sorts of vicious and lascivious thoughts, for quarrels and many kinds of foolishness. These make a man, in the words of Elihu, act as if he had a bellyful of new wine which needs vent and which will burst the vessels into which it is put.[82] And when a man who has been intent all day on empty show and listening to gossip, recollects himself at last, it is only to find that he has brought a host of frivolous images to his soul, which trouble his conscience and even drive away his sleep with fevered dreams. Thus his prayers are constantly interrupted by thoughts of adventures and battles, and knights and kings.

And there is yet another, a more evil type of curiosity, which belongs especially to those who have some degree of virtue. I mean the temptation to prove their worth by working miracles, which is simply tempting God, and was prohibited in the law of Moses. *Thou shalt not tempt the Lord thy God*,[83] we read, and Saint Paul says the same: *Neither let us tempt Christ.*[84] This horrible vice may bring about a dreadful punishment, for instance if the miracle worker does not achieve what he had hoped for and should commit the sin of despair through his disappointment, or should incur the sacrilege of blasphemy.

23

Vanity

Now we come to the third branch of the evil root which the Apostle calls the pride of life. There are many kinds of pride, but here we shall consider only two of them: firstly the love of praise, and secondly the desire to lord it over others. And who shall say how much trouble these can give, good Lord? When, for instance, I am upset by a correction or an insult, or by some detraction or contradiction, or if I am downcast by sadness, I shall, when I look for the cause of this, find it deeply hidden away in the lowest roots of vanity. Because of this deep-seated vanity, I have thought great things of myself, and am now downcast because I see that my self-estimate was completely false. And yet I have no wish to be corrected or blamed. All I wish for is praise or honour from the lips of all my acquaintances.

When the soul is infected by this poison, we quite often think to ourselves that other people esteem us holy, and as soon as we see that we are mistaken even in this, we give way to depression and misery. And we are always on the look-out so as to have the first place wherever we sit in company, to receive the first greeting, and to have our opinion sought first. The more our whims are pandered to, the more we like it, and the more furious we become when our wishes are denied.

24

The desire for power

THE degree to which the soul may be corrupted by the lust for power can be told only by those who have known it themselves, and who have subsequently been delivered from it by the help of God's grace. Its first effect is to make us servile towards those who we think will help us to realize our own schemes. With no heed for the truth we will praise the things they praise, and blame the things they blame. We will be jealous of others who come nearer than us to the familiar friendship of those in power, and we shall be so consumed by envy that we are unable to eat or sleep properly.

From this it is but a short step to spreading detraction and malicious rumours about others. And if we are supplanted altogether by someone cleverer than ourselves, what torments we have then to suffer! Once aroused, our ambition must have some victim when we are disappointed of our hopes, and so our words and even our silences are full of bitterness and indignation. Our speech and manner become harsh, truculent and argumentative. And then, when we know that our hope is lost, we change altogether in our manner towards those whose favour we once went to such pains to acquire. We have nothing good to say about them now, nothing but contradictions, insults and malicious suggestions to offer. We can see no good in anything they do, and we subject every word they say to an unkind interpretation, being always on the look-out for some slight or double-dealing. And if we can pretend that it is the zeal for God's service that motivates us, we manage to work up tears and sighs as we denounce them for all manner of evil-doing.

It were better, of course, that in religious communities those who are rebellious and contumacious should be expelled from the society of those whose life they make a misery. All societies should, ideally, be ruled by those who can obey rules, and who are themselves humble, quiet and reasonable. But in fact it only too often happens that those most ill-suited to govern are put in positions of power simply to keep them quiet, and to stop them getting completely out of hand—a lamentable state of affairs!

But I think we have, by now, said sufficient on the matter of the threefold concupiscence. And reading through these chapters, we may, perhaps, see our own faces. And if we see there any deformity or ugliness, or anything that is not as it should be, the light of truth will help us to discern the cause of the blemishes that we find. We shall blame our own perverseness and not the harshness of the Lord's yoke, for indeed it is not harsh at all. The roots of our passions are the things that cause all the trouble, and if we can cast them out, we shall find that our shoulders feel no burden under the Lord's yoke. We shall learn from Him how to be meek and humble of heart, and we shall thus find rest for our souls. We shall celebrate a Sabbath rest that is not just one day in our temporal lives, as the Jews understood it, but an eternal Sabbath, a Sabbath for our souls in the delights of true charity.

I

The three Sabbaths

IN this third part we will take as our guide the three Sabbaths of which we read in the book of Leviticus.[1] In the Old Law the Israelites were commanded to rest on three different occasions. First of all there was the seventh day, then the seventh year, and thirdly the sabbatical year which came every fifty years, namely at the end of seven times seven years. The first was a Sabbath of days, the second a Sabbath of years, and the third one might call a Sabbath of Sabbaths. The latter came always as an additional year to the seven Sabbaths of forty-nine years, bringing the number seven to a concluding unity. Unity thus brought the cycle to an end, which had begun in unity, namely with the first year that the Hebrews counted. Every good work, indeed, begins with faith in the one true God, and it develops under the aegis of the Holy Spirit with His seven gifts, so that it may be brought to fulfilment in God, who is truly One. In Him, we are made one with Him. And since there is no division in true unity, we must take care not to let our minds and hearts be distracted by this or that, but simply to be at one in God who is One. Let all be in Him, and about Him; through Him and with Him. Let us know Him alone, and enjoy Him alone, and being always one in Him, we shall always be at rest in Him, celebrating our perpetual Sabbath.

For the moment we have only a foretaste of this Sabbath of Sabbaths, whereas we already know and enjoy the

Sabbath of days and the Sabbath of years. But who shall speak of these various Sabbaths in any way transcending what anyone may read in the Scriptures? Who is there, sufficiently enlightened by the Spirit of God, to speak of these things from his own experience? Come then, good Jesus, come to Thy poor servant who begs for crumbs. He looks for nothing from the rich man's table, but, like a dog, he waits at his master's board for whatever may fall from it. And his master, in this case, is none other than Moses, who feasted royally at Thy table. Thou hast said, kind Lord, that it is not a good thing for the bread of Thy sons to be thrown to dogs, but none the less the dogs were in fact allowed to eat up the scraps that were thrown to them, and so I know that bread will be broken even for me. And when the bread is too hard for me, do Thou break it into crumbs.

2

Three kinds of love

LET us first listen to the words of Him who breaks the bread for us: *Thou shalt love the Lord thy God with thy whole heart and with thy whole soul and with thy whole mind. Thou shalt love thy neighbour as thyself. On these two commandments depend the whole law and the prophets.*[2] If we believe the truth, or rather because we believe, we must find the reason for distinguishing three Sabbaths in these two commandments, for they themselves are part of the law. If you consider these commandments carefully, you will see that we are commanded to love ourselves, our fellow men, and God. If we are told that we must love our neighbour as ourselves, then obviously we have to love ourselves. This is hardly of precept, because it is something inborn in our nature. As Saint Paul says, no one ever hated his own flesh,[3] and what is true of the flesh must be even truer of the mind of man, for no man ever loved his body more than his mind, whatever he might suppose to the contrary. Given the choice, everyone would prefer to suffer from sickness of the body rather than lose his reason.

We will consider a man's natural love of himself, then, as our first Sabbath. The love of our fellow men shall be the second Sabbath, and the love of God, the Sabbath of Sabbaths. A spiritual Sabbath, as we have already remarked, is tranquillity of mind, and peace and rest in the heart. Only in the love of God do we find such a fulfilment of rest, but we do none the less find it sometimes in pleasant brotherly love, and even occasionally in the love of ourselves. This is when we love ourselves in the manner that God wishes, and when we love our fellow men as we love ourselves. We must love ourselves and our fellow men because the love of God commands it, but whereas we are commanded to love our neighbour as ourself, we must love God *more* than our neighbour and more than ourselves.

We shall consider in due course, God willing, how we are to love our fellow men, but for the moment I would like you to consider how the three kinds of love of which we are speaking here, are so bound to one another that unless we love God we cannot love our neighbour, and unless we love ourselves we cannot love our neighbour as ourselves. In other words, each one of these three kinds of love depends on the others, and in each one of the three we find the other two. We cannot have one unless we have all three, and if we lose one we lose them all. *He who loves not his brother whom he sees, how can he love God whom he sees not?*[4] Saint John asks. From this angle it would appear that the love of our neighbour is a necessary condition of our love of God, just as we must love ourselves before we can love our fellow men. In either case the precedence is one of order. It does not mean that the love which comes first is the greater. The two lesser loves precede the one of which it is written: *Thou shalt love the Lord thy God with thy whole heart and with thy whole mind and with thy whole soul.*[5]

If we do not love God, on the other hand, our love for our neighbour is dead, even non-existent. It seems to me that our love for God is the life-giving spirit which enables the other loves to exist, and without which they cannot be. We cannot truly love ourselves unless we first love God, nor can we love our neighbour unless God increases our capacity for loving. The love of God is like a fire in our hearts that burns brighter and brighter, and the sparks that fly out from it are the lesser loves, which belong to it and fall back into the fullness of the flame. It is a fire that carries us up with it to the supreme goodness of God, in which all lesser love is turned into the love of God. There we cannot say that we love ourselves or our fellow men as such, for we love them with a love that is wholly devoted to God, since we are unable to see anything but Himself.

These three loves are conceived one by another; they give each other fervour and increase. All of them are made perfect together, as one. This comes about in a wonderful way that is beyond our comprehension. Although we possess these three kinds of love together—for they cannot be had separately—we are not conscious of them all the time to the same degree. At one moment we may be extremely aware of the peace and the joy that goes with one particular Sabbath, and at another time we shall feel differently. Sometimes we shall be specially aware of the peace in our own souls, whilst at other times we shall be more conscious of the happiness that comes of brotherly love. Sometimes we shall have that greatest of all joys which is only found in the contemplation of God. We are rather like those opulent kings who keep stores of aromatic spices, simply for the pleasure of smelling now this one, now that one. Our soul is a storehouse of spiritual riches, and in it we can take our pleasure and enjoy whatever most delights us, as we consider the variety of the glorious things that are ours.

3

The first Sabbath, which is the love of oneself

WHEN a man goes in, as it were, to the secret place of his soul, turning his back on all the noise and worry and vanity of the outside world, he shuts the door and looks around, and what does he find? Here all is at peace, all is in order. There is nothing to cause remorse. Everything gives him joy, and conduces to calm. Like a well ordered family, all his thoughts, words and deeds are gathered about him, and he can smile on them benevolently like a father in a disciplined household. And this gives rise in his heart to a wonderful sense of security, and his security gives him such a joy and happiness, that he cannot but thank and praise God the more fervently for His blessings. This is the seventh day of rest that is only made possible by six days of labour, for we must expend our energy in good works before we can take our rest with a peaceful conscience. A clear conscience is born of zealous works, and we cannot love ourselves unless we have a good conscience. Whoever does evil, and loves evil, cannot love his own soul. But whoever loves goodness and acts with justice, does indeed love his soul. And this is the joyful solemnity of our first day of rest, on which day we put aside servile works, forbearing to light the fire of lust and casting down the burden of our passions.

4

The Sabbath of brotherly love

WHEN we have celebrated our first Sabbath in the peace of
our own hearts, we can go on to consider how this heart of
ours must be enlarged, so as to become a great hospice in
which to welcome all those who need our sympathy when
they are sorrowful, or who would have us rejoice with
them when they are glad. If our brethren are weak, we
must be weak with them, and when they are scandalized,
so must we be likewise. Each of us must feel in his soul
how charity binds him to each one of his fellow men.
There must be no room in our hearts for envy or indignation, for suspicion or moroseness. On the contrary, we
must gather all the world to our hearts to share in our peace,
and embrace and cherish our fellow men so as to have one
heart and one mind with them all. In our hearts there will
be absolute peace from everything evil and vicious and
selfish, as we rest in the gentle enjoyment of brotherly love.
In this Sabbath we have the guidance of one who enjoyed
it to the full, namely Saint Paul, who tells us: *Thou shalt
not commit adultery; Thou shalt not steal; Thou shalt not bear
false witness, and if there be any other commandment, it is com-
prised in this word: Thou shalt love thy neighbour as thyself.*[6]
We also have the prophet David to sing to us in a joyful
strain: *Behold how good and how pleasant it is for brethren to
dwell together in unity.*[7] How good indeed, and how very
pleasant! It is good, because it is more useful than any other
thing. It is pleasant, because nothing is more enjoyable.

The first Sabbath was a single day of rest, and the soul's
Sabbath that corresponds to it, is the peace that a man enjoys
in his own conscience. But now we have a whole year
consecrated to Sabbath rest, and just as a year is composed
of many days, so is the second Sabbath of the spirit a welding

together of many souls and many hearts into one, in the fire of charity. And if we would draw a mystical meaning from the fact that this spiritual Sabbath must be preceded by six foregoing years, it is surely this. There are six different sorts and conditions of men towards which we must exercise the virtue of love. Each year is composed of many days, and each one of these sorts of men will join to us many members by the bond of love.

First of all our love is of its natural ordering directed to those who are bound to us by family ties. This love is part of our human nature, and if we lacked it we would not be human. Indeed, Saint Paul says: *If any man have not care of his own, and especially those of his house, he has denied the faith and is worse than an infidel.* Nor are we to think that this is a contradiction of Our Lord's words, when He says that whoever comes to Him, and does not hate mother and father and even his own life, cannot be a disciple.[8] But we shall go into this later. If we do not have a care for our own, and especially of those of our own house, we shall certainly find that many true lovers will find their Sabbath rest before we do. God said that we must honour our fathers and mothers,[9] so it is clear that God has set the seal of His law, by means of a commandment, on what is already an instinct of our nature.

Next we come to the love of our friends, and of those to whom we are connected through ties of duty. This is a more general love, applied to more persons than the love of our blood relations. But even this is no greater than the justice of the Pharisees, who loved their friends and hated their enemies.[10] Granted that there is no great merit in either of these sorts of affection, since they are instinct in our nature, none the less the natural law impels us to love our relatives, whereas the love of our friends is something to which grace calls us, for if we neglect it, we bring about our own condemnation. *If you love them that love you, what*

86

reward shall you have? Do not even the publicans do this? And if you salute your brethren only, what do you more? Do not also the heathens this?[11] In order then that our affection should be directed to something greater, we embrace also those who are connected with us by holding the same beliefs and living according to them. This love will certainly have a reward because God is the reason for our showing it.

We are called Christians because we follow Christ, and Christ means 'the anointed one'. Now we share in Our Lord's anointing, precisely through this sort of love. You remember that Aaron was anointed so that the oil ran down his beard, even to the skirts of his clothing. This love gives us a share in Our Lord's anointing. It is as if it brought us into some physical contact with Him, as if our clothes touched the anointed clothes of Jesus, whom Aaron prefigures. Whoever shares this anointing shares that particular quality of Jesus that His name denotes, and thus sharing we can do as He does, gathering our fellow men to our hearts.

Next we must consider two more sorts of men who, if we can learn to love them truly, will help us on our way to the Sabbath we desire. These are they who stand outside Holy Church, Jews and Gentiles, the heretics and schismatics whose ignorance must cause us pain, whose weakness we must compassionate, whose wickedness we must weep over, and for whose comfort and conversion we must pray with a genuine tenderness. Our desire must be that they may one day be with us, in Jesus Christ our Lord.

Finally there is that love, the sixth in this reckoning, in which brotherly love finds its highest fulfilment, the image of God's goodness in us comes to its absolute perfection, and we are made truly Sons of God. *'Love your enemies'*, Our Lord said. *'Do good to them that hate you, and pray for them that persecute and calumniate you, that you may be the children of your Father who is in heaven.'*[12] What can we do more than this? Surely nothing remains but the Sabbath year, in which no creditor may ask for what is owed him, and slaves are given their freedom ! Whoever has learned to look on his enemies with gentleness, can sincerely pray, *'Forgive us our debts, as we also forgive our debtors'*.[13] Whoever commits sin, is the slave of sin,[14] but when he has learned to love and forgive others, he is himself forgiven and loved. He is not only restored to freedom, but he becomes a friend to his fellow men. Then all is at peace for him, all is gentleness, and happiness and rejoicing about him. When our likeness to God is thus restored to us there is no place for sorrow, no reason for anxiety and trouble to spoil our joy. By then we have come the whole way from that first Sabbath, which we enjoyed in the fruits of our labours in our own souls, and we can love all mankind in the fullness of our affection. We can remain unmoved by injuries that are done to us, and like understanding parents, we can consider our enemies as children who need our patience in their infirmities. Indeed the more injury they do to us, the more we realize their need for compassion and the more love we can give them. Whoever can love to this degree can celebrate the greatest Sabbath of all, for he has learned how good and joyful a thing it is for brothers to live at one with each other. He knows the sweetness of brotherly love, and he can count all men his dearest friends.

5

The love of God is a safeguard for all other loves

As we have already agreed, the love which unites us to our brethren, and the love we bear towards ourselves for our own salvation, must have in them something of the love of God to give them life. It is the love of God that gives every other love its impulse. Now the proper love of ourselves and the love of our fellow men give us back our innocence, and innocence consists of two things. First of all it means that we do ourselves no harm, and secondly that we do no harm to our neighbour. We do injury to ourselves by indulging in the vices that corrupt our flesh, but these we can learn to shun if we will only consider the human flesh which our Saviour took, when he became man, for love of us. *The Word was made flesh and dwelt amongst us.*[15] We can eschew the pleasures of the flesh if we are in the habit of thinking on Our Lord in every facet of His humanity, from His great dignity in heaven to His humble birth in a poor stable. We can think of Him nestling at His mother's breast. We can see Him fondled in Mary's arms, caressed by the trembling hands of old Simeon,[16] and kissed by his grateful lips. Whoever loves to think of these things will often dwell on Our Lord's meekness and the kindness of His words; His compassion on sinners, on the wretched and the sick. What wonderful goodness He showed us in going to eat with publicans, and in allowing Himself to be touched by a woman of evil life.[17] Remember that he defended a woman taken in adultery from those who wished to stone her, and that He spoke with such gentleness to another that she who had once been an adulteress became an evangelist, bearing His good news to others.[18] Now if we consider what a wonderful picture Our Lord makes as He befriends these poor souls, do we not find that all the delights of the flesh turn into so much filth? It is such considerations as this that bring the tears easily to our eyes, putting out the fire of lust that burns in us, cooling our flesh, tempering our appetites, and quietening every incentive to vanity.

But the perfection of brotherly love is of course in the love we bear towards those who hate us, and nothing can give so much incentive to our striving after this virtue as the remembrance of the way in which Our Lord bore His sufferings. He was more beautiful than all the sons of men,[19] but He did not turn away His face from those who spat at Him. Those eyes, which were the eyes of God, seeing and ruling over all things, He allowed to be darkened by evil men. His body He gave to be scourged. His head, the very sight of which made Powers and Principalities bow down in reverence, He bent low to be crowned by piercing thorns. He submitted to insult and suffering, the nails, the cross, the lance, the bitter drink, and all the while He was gentle and calm and loving. Like a lamb led to the slaughter, He kept silent.[20]

Let worldly men, and all those who are proud and arrogant, take note of all this suffering. Let us think who it is that suffered thus, and how much He suffered, and what were His torments. Let us think on them deeply, for I cannot write about them in any way which can do them justice. All that I can say is that no man can conceive such patience as Our Lord showed, without anger leaving his soul forthwith. Only to hear those words, *Father, forgive them for they know not what they do,*[21] spoken in a voice of infinite gentleness and love and peace makes our hearts go out even to those who hate us. *Father, forgive them. . . .* What further love and gentleness could be added to His prayer? They crucify Him, but they do not know who it is that they are crucifying. If they had known they would never have put to death the Lord of glory.[22] Therefore, Our Lord prays, *Father, forgive them . . . !* His murderers believe Him to be a transgressor of the law, a seducer of the people, a blasphemous upstart who claims to be equal to God in divinity. But Our Lord has hidden His face from them, so that they cannot recognize His divine majesty. And so they must be forgiven, for they do not know what they are doing.

We have seen, then, that if we wish to love ourselves in the way God wants us to love ourselves, we must not be corrupted by the pleasures of the flesh. And in order that we be not overcome by these pleasures, the remedy is to turn all our love of the flesh to the flesh of Our Blessed Lord. Finally, in order to reach the state of perfect love for our fellow men, we must take even our enemies to our hearts. But we cannot remain in this perfect state unless we think always of the patience of Our Blessed Lord and Saviour in His sufferings.

6

The perfect Sabbath in the love of God

WHEN we have been purified by the twofold love of which we have just treated, we can find our way into God's own sanctuary and be embraced by Him there. Our longing breaks through the limitations of our flesh, and there we see Jesus Christ as God. We are drawn into His glorious light, and lost in His unbelievable joy. Everything that belongs to our human nature, everything fleshly and perceptible and transitory is stilled. All we can do is to gaze on the One who is forever changeless, and as we gaze on Him, we are perfectly at rest; so great is the delight we find in His embrace that this is indeed the Sabbath of all Sabbaths. This is the year of jubilee, during which every man returns to his possession,[23] by which we are to understand that we return to our Maker, to whom we belong, and who is Himself our greatest possession. We belong to Him and He belongs to us. He holds us in His embrace, and we cling fast to Him. He is the choice possession which we sold by our sins, when we turned away from Him and gave our love to lesser things. Once we prized the creatures of God more highly than their creator. But in the fiftieth year, the year of Sabbath, servile fear is no more. Not only does the lust of the flesh fade away, but even the memory of it, as the spirit comes into its own.

Before Pentecost the Spirit was not bestowed on men, for Jesus was not yet glorified.[24] By this we understand, not that the Spirit had not been given at all, but that He had not been fully and completely given. The Spirit had certainly been given on the first Sabbath, and again on the second, but on the Sabbath of Sabbaths His fullness was poured out. In the first two sabbaths the Spirit could not be fully given because Jesus was not yet glorified. Far from seeing Him in glory, we contemplated Him in His humiliations. We saw Him, not as a great king, but as a little child in His mother's arms. But when charity is poured out in our hearts, it can only be through the Holy Spirit who is given to us.[25] It is the Holy Spirit who comes to us with His seven gifts, but seven times seven gifts must mean the very perfection and fulfilment of all that He can give. The seventh day is the beginning of charity, the seventh year is its development, and the fiftieth year its fullness. In each Sabbath we find rest and peace and joy for the spirit, but the first belongs to a man's own quiet conscience, the second to a community of men living happily together, and the third consists in the contemplation of God. The first sabbath is rest from sin, the second is rest from cupidity and the third is rest from every sort of dissension. In the first one we taste and see how sweet the manhood of Jesus is. In the second we see how perfect and complete is His charity. In the third we see Him as He is in Himself, as God. First we are recollected in our own souls, then we are drawn to the love of our fellow men, and finally we are lifted up to heaven.

7

Love, charity and cupidity

AT this point we should consider in a little more detail how charity is to be manifested in the Christian life, but before we can do this we must define a little more closely what we mean by charity. Charity is obviously love, but it is equally obvious that not all love is charity. So first of all we must ascertain what love is, because we cannot find the species until we have found the genus.[26] Love can be taken in two ways. First of all it can be that natural instinct in the soul by means of which it is natural for the soul to love. Notice that I speak of an instinct, not of a faculty. Secondly it can be the soul's act of loving, which means that it is *using* its native impulse to love. The act, or our use of the impulse to love, can be a good or a bad one, in so far as we love something we ought or ought not to love. Thus we speak of love plus something else—the love of money or the love of wisdom, and these are either good or bad according to their object. But the impulse to love, which brings about acts of love whether good or bad, is in itself something good. Whether it turns to good or evil, it can never be evil in itself, but only good. This is because it is a part of human nature, which was made good by God, who is infinitely good Himself, and who made all things not only good, but very good. Man, however, is endowed with a free will, and although this, like everything else created in him, is good, none the less he either uses it for good if he is helped by grace, or for evil if he acts unaided by God's grace. Whether our habits are good or evil depends on our love, or rather on the object of our affections. The good use of good things makes us good, because it produces a good love in us. But the abuse of good things gives rise to bad love, and makes us bad in consequence. Therefore we may define charity as the good use of love, and cupidity, its opposite, as the abuse of love.

8

The right and wrong uses of love

LET us now see what distinguishes the good and bad uses of love in fuller detail. As I see it, love is used in three human acts, namely in the choice of an object to love, in our movement towards that object, and in the enjoyment of the same. We make our choice by using our reason. We move towards what we want by means of desire and action, while our enjoyment comes as the term of this whole process. We who are endowed with reason have a natural capacity for beatitude which is part of our nature. We were made with it, and we are always hungry for happiness, but we can never find sufficient enjoyment in ourselves. And unfortunately the things which, later on, we discover to be insufficient for our enjoyment, we seize upon under the impression that these are our true beatitude. Anything will do so long as it is something other than ourselves ! This is how we place our beatitude in things, or the enjoyment of things, either because we are mistaken, or deceived by the senses, or deficient in faith or intelligence. And this is what we choose as the object of our beatitude, and set out to attain, because we think it can make us happy. Love, the impulse in our nature of which we have already spoken, makes this choice. Or we can say that the reason makes this choice by means of that impulse, for love always has reason for its companion. This does not mean that we always love reasonably. It simply means that we distinguish

94

clearly between what we choose and what we reject. Reason can see the difference between creature and Creator, temporal and eternal, sweet and bitter, pleasant and unpleasant, and love chooses from among these.

Choice is an act of the soul, and it also can be called love. But although love itself, which is making the choice, is always good, choice on the contrary can be either good or bad. And in this way we can speak of love also being good or bad. We may choose something that is not for us, either because we have already formed an attraction to it by previous experience, or because we are inexperienced and make a false judgement. The result is unhappiness for us in our love for that particular object. Enjoyment means the use of something that gives pleasure and joy in the using. At the moment when we make our choice, love moves towards the object we have chosen, filling the soul with desire and carrying it towards that object. This movement of desire is also known as love, and if the object of our choice is something that God wishes us to have, then our love is good. If not, it is bad. Finally, when we have achieved the desired object, we can take pleasure in it and enjoy it. Thus charity and greed both comprise the three acts of choice, pursuit and enjoyment. Choice is the beginning of love, whether it be good or bad love. The progress of love consists in doing all that can be done to attain what it wants, while at the end of our efforts comes enjoyment or fruition of what we sought.

Charity means that in the first place we have chosen something we are permitted to have; that we have gone about attaining it in the right way, and that having attained it we enjoy it in the way that God meant it to be enjoyed. Charity implies a wise choice and an enjoyment that will benefit us. It begins as a choice, it develops as the pursuit of something good, and comes to its term in enjoyment.

But if we choose unwisely, and seek what we have chosen in a wrongful manner, and end by abusing what we have acquired, this is greed, and the root of all evil. But charity is the root of all that is good.

9

The choice of good

HAVING distinguished between good and bad love, it now remains for us to see what we must choose for our enjoyment, and how we have to go about attaining it. We must find out, in other words, what is to be loved, and how it is to be loved. We do not, indeed, love everything that we choose, but only those things that we select for our use and enjoyment. If we are held fast in the dungheap of the flesh, we shall aspire to nothing higher than trumpery wealth, useless honours, worldly favours, or the pleasures of the body, a false idea of happiness persuading us that such things can constitute a satisfactory aim for the soul. There are various ways of enjoying these things. One man will be a merchant and another an artisan; one a soldier and another a thief. But only a man who chooses worldly aims in order to enjoy them, can truly be said to love them. The rest of men only use those things as means to some further end. The crooked mind of man imagines it can find happiness in enjoyment, as long as the desired object is not yet possessed, but as soon as it is possessed man falls back on his own emptiness, and realizes that his efforts have been in vain. Then he is filled by the desire to run after something else, and again he repeats his disappointment.

But if we lead a pure life and our soul is pure and wholesome, and our vision clear, we will look into the matter with an enlightened mind and see that no one is sufficient to

himself in the matter of happiness, and that the love of
things beneath us will drag us down with them instead of
lifting us up, giving us only misery and never consolation.
We will make a true estimate of ourselves and take note
that our true privilege lies in God's command that we love
and serve Him only.[27] God would never have said this if
there had been anyone but Himself higher than we, who
could give us happiness and to whom we owed reverence.
Therefore we must choose God above all things so that we
may enjoy Him, and this choice is the beginning of true
love. Desiring Him above all others, brings about the
development of love. And our love will be perfect because
we love only the perfect good, and our beatitude likewise
will be complete. Rightly it was, then, that the divine law
gave as the first and greatest commandment: *Thou shalt love
the Lord thy God.*[28] The commandment to love God is the
first and the greatest of all the commandments, and when
we secure for ourselves this greatest of all good, containing
all our happiness, we shall enjoy it to the fullness of our
powers. And rightly enough the second commandment is
Thou shalt love thy neighbour, for clearly the capacity of all
men together in loving God is greater than the capacity of
any one individual. There will be greater happiness for
those whose capacity is less, if they can make their own what
is possessed by others whose capacity is greater. But of
course we cannot have the divine goodness that others have
in themselves, unless we love both them and the goodness
in them.

God is our highest good, in Himself, in us, and in each
other, and therefore He is wholly to be loved with all our
heart and soul and strength. *Thou shalt love thy neighbour as
thyself* means that our neighbour's good must cause us as
much happiness as our own. And so we must choose both
God and our neighbour, but not in the same way. God we
must choose for His own sake, and in order that we may

enjoy Him as He is in Himself. But we must choose our neighbour so as to enjoy him in God and to enjoy God in him. Now I grant that this word 'enjoy' is normally used in a more restricted sense and applied to God alone, but remember that Paul, when writing to Philemon, prayed *that I may enjoy thee in the Lord.*[29] When our reason can agree that these two, God and our neighbour, are both to be chosen, and all else set aside, our love of God and our love of our neighbour have made a real beginning, for it means that love has turned in the direction that God requires it to take.

10

Love moves us to desire and to action

I HAVE now said sufficient about choice to be able to go on to consider the direction that love takes. Love can move inwardly and thus become desire, or outwardly, when it becomes action. The direction we call desire means that our appetite is awakened in respect to the object we have chosen for our enjoyment. The outward direction implies that an external act is to be undertaken to reach that object, the soul's instinctive love commanding the act. And so I think the next thing we have to think about is precisely what the incentives are which move love in these two directions, what the directions are, and precisely what they determine. Then we can go on to discuss how far we may let ourselves be guided by these compelling movements, for it may be necessary at times to acquiesce, and at other times to ignore them, or to adapt them by increasing or diminishing their power.

The two movements in question, the inward movement of desire, and the outward movement of action, are commanded either by reason or attraction, sometimes by one or other separately, and sometimes by both together. Reason tells us that we must choose both God and our fellow men for our enjoyment, and so we must now see how love must move us in the direction of our choice. Then we can think of all the other various directions that love may take.

II

Love and attraction

WE may define attraction as a spontaneous inclination of the soul that gives pleasure. It can be spiritual, rational or irrational; it can be an attraction towards our friends or our relatives, or on the lowest level, merely to the carnal side of nature. The soul is moved by a spiritual attraction when in some mysterious and unexpected way the Holy Spirit comes to it, giving a taste of that sweetness which comes to us in our love for God and for our fellow men. We have already gone into the manner and the cause of these visitations of the Holy Spirit.[30] The contrary of this attraction comes, of course, from the devil, the spirit of fornication deceiving men by drawing them to shameful acts. This fire in the flesh and the sowing of thoughts of delight and pleasure in the mind, weakening its resistance to evil, are the two great torments of souls who strive to be virtuous.

David's son, Amnon, unless I am mistaken, was thus overcome by the devil, who filled his heart with desire for his sister. And the result of this was that dishonour was brought on that great house, the girl's brothers revenged themselves on her seducer, and it gave rise to the occasion for Absalom to covet his father's power.[31] There is no need to be surprised if I call this a 'spiritual' attraction, for it is brought about by vices which are of a spiritual kind.

Rational and irrational attraction

A RATIONAL attraction is one that we conceive through observing the virtues of others. It may be virtuous conduct that we see or read or hear about; in all cases it causes us a particular sort of joy. It is the attraction we experience towards the martyrs in their fortitude, their triumphs over torture. It fills us with admiration and devotion to them, and with shame and sorrow for our own sinfulness. It is as if we saw them with our own eyes, as we meditate on their lives. . . . St. Paul's for instance, whose deeds are so readily commended to us through his words, moving us to tears. Who, when reading of Paul's perils in the sea and from thieves, from his own people and from the gentiles,[32] does not at the same time recall the secret of his power? Everywhere, and in all things, he says, he is instructed both to be full and to be hungry, both to have ample and to suffer need. 'I can do all things in him that strengthens me.'[33] Who, when hearing these words, or reading them, would not be moved towards a real love for the one who wrote them?

It was this kind of attraction that existed between David and Jonathan, binding and consecrating the first fruits of a most holy love. The bond of charity between them was so strong that Jonathan's father could not break it. Such was David's fortitude when he killed the giant Goliath—and thus gave reason for Jonathan's father to envy him—that it would have been a wonderful example to Jonathan that he would never forget. Jonathan's soul was bound to David's, for since he was a lover of virtue, he could not but love the one in whom great virtue shone, and so he loved David as he loved his own soul.[34] And this is the attraction which Our merciful Lord Himself exercised on that young man who was in admiration of His great virtues, for we are told that the youth was attracted to Him and that Our Lord, looking on him, loved him.

The contrary of this attraction is of course irrational, being the kind of fascination exercised by vicious people, vain philosophers and bragging, foolhardy soldiers. And what is even worse, there can be an attraction exercised by sensual and evil-living men, wastrels and seducers, and those who spend all their time in vain show, and those who patronize and condone evil-doers.

13

The attraction of friendship

It is obvious that we must be kindly disposed to those to whom we do some service, and likewise gratitude makes those attractive to us who do us kindnesses. There are various examples in Holy Scripture to illustrate what I mean. Remember, for instance, how Moses fled from Pharaoh, and made his dwelling in Madian,[35] where the priest made a friend of him by giving him one of his daughters. And this in itself was a return of gratitude for a service which Moses rendered him when he protected those seven daughters from the importunity of the shepherds. The priest took Moses to himself, not as a friend only, but also as a son-in-law. Then there was Berzellai the Galaadite who received David kindly and gave him everything he needed when he was fleeing in distress from Absalom.[36] And this kindness David remembered to the end of his days with gratitude, giving among his last orders to Solomon the decree that there should always be room at the king's table for the sons of Berzellai.[37]

The ties of kindred

IN the first place, we all have a natural inclination to cherish those who are near to us by the ties of the flesh, and indeed no one ever hated his own flesh,[38] nor can a mother forget her own child.[39] If anyone should neglect the members of his own household, he would be denying the faith, being no better than a heathen.[40] The love of one's own family we find among the holiest of men, as for instance, the patriarchs of the Old Testament who would bind their sons by an oath to bury them with their forefathers in their native land.[41] We find it also exemplified in that wisest of men, King Solomon, who knew which of the two women was lying when they came each to claim the same child as her own.[42] The real mother's love declared itself in praying the king to give the child to the woman who had no feeling for it at all, rather than have it cut in two. One said, *I pray thee give her the child alive, and let it not be killed,* while the other said, *Neither mine nor thine, but let it be divided.*

Again in the story of Joseph, we read that he wept to see the trouble his brothers were in[43] when they made their tardy repentance for having sold him into slavery as a boy. David too, remembering that he was Absalom's father, even when his son was trying to kill him, forgot the injury his son intended to do to him and prayed his followers, *Save me the boy.*[44]

Finally we remember how our blessed Lord lamented over His own city of Jerusalem in His compassion,[45] knowing it would soon be destroyed.[46] Also we think of Paul who modelled his life on that of the Master, and preferred to be anathema from Christ for the sake of his brethren according to the flesh.[47]

Carnal attraction

WE may consider two sorts of carnal attraction. Firstly there is our inclination towards others on account of their external appearance, without any connotation of particular virtue or vice. It is easy indeed to see why we should be attracted to those who are beautiful to look at, well made in body, well spoken, and distinguished in their behaviour. Even though we have no idea who a man may be, or what he may be, yet his appearance speaks volumes, and we find him appealing because of it. This was the pleasing quality that endeared Moses to Pharaoh's daughter, just as it had done to his own parents who even kept him for three months despite Pharaoh's orders that all Hebrew boys should be murdered. *They saw he was a comely babe, and they feared not the King's edict.*[48] Because the child's beauty pleased her, Pharaoh's daughter brought him up and made him one of the great men of the king's court. Such an attraction as this, as we said, has no particular virtue or vice in it. At the same time we have to admit that the attraction exercised by a beautiful person can move us to lust as well as love. David saw Bethsabee when he was walking on the roof of his palace while she was bathing.[49] Temptation took him by surprise and brought him into great sorrow, leading him not only to take another man's wife but also to destroy that very man because of her. Even the wise Solomon was overcome by the attraction of beautiful women, who led him to a worse idolatry than that of the flesh, for he joined also in the worship of their false gods.[50]

What we are to think of these attractions

These, as we said, are the origins of love, the roots of love. They cannot themselves rightly be called love. To be moved by such attractions, if they are good, we do not regard as greatly virtuous; nor, if they are bad, are they greatly destructive. The good attraction can be turned by a man to his own ruin, and the bad (which is usually considered to be so very much worse) can be considered as a trial, making good men stronger to resist evil in the future, after a momentary fall.

These attractions do not themselves lead us, but they do guide us, and in the measure in which they guide us we judge them to be good or bad. If their guidance is bad, we call it temptation; and if it is good, we can call it an inspiration. When we are moved to act under the impulse of these attractions, it means that the will has given its full consent, although this consent is not always manifested in the outward act. It can remain as an inward desire. Now we have to see how far we may allow love to be guided by our attraction to others. But before we do this we must examine the part played by reason, which is yet another guide for the soul in its choice of what to love.

17

Reason impels us to love God and our fellow men

Even though we may not feel a great deal of love towards our fellow men, or even towards God, reason insists that we make the necessary effort to love. Reason convinces us that we must so act not only because it is to our advantage or use, but because God and our neighbour are worthy of our love. That God must be loved is clear enough in our minds, because we know that the love of God is necessary and good for us and that it is a worthy object to pursue. It is necessary, if we would be saved from damnation. It is good for us since it is the means of our glorification. It is worthy of us because God first loved us, and therefore we must love Him in return. We must desire God because He is our good, and without Him we must be for ever wretched. He for His part, needing nothing from us, was willing to forgo all happiness for our sake, and now with Him we can be only perfectly happy.

If we accept these truths, even in our minds only, and without the full consent of the heart, desire for God will grow even in our hesitant love. And if we wish to attain what we desire, we are all the more zealous to fulfil God's commands, for they are the means to the end we have in view. Now the greatest commandment for us is that we consider our neighbour as ourselves. Reason therefore insists that we do good to him. Our fellow men must always fall into three categories. Either they are friends or enemies, or something between these two, neither friends nor enemies. A man is a friend to us either because he is good to us now, or was good in the past. If he is not near to us by some blood tie, he is certainly near to us if he has done us a kind service. An enemy is obviously someone who has done, or is doing us harm. And if a man is neither friend nor enemy to us, this means that he has done us no injury, and that is all we know about him.

Now reason commands that we do good to our friends, not only because we are commanded to do so, nor because it comes naturally to us to do so, but because they have a right to expect it of us if we are real friends. We love our enemy for the simple reason that God commands us to. We must love the man who is neither friend nor enemy, because, again, we are commanded to love our neighbour.

We must follow the dictates of reason in all these matters, and be prepared to do good to enemy and friend alike. We may feel no love towards our enemy, but we shall none the less be showing real charity towards him.

18

A distinction between two loves

WE have then to distinguish between love in our reason and love in our inclinations. We often hesitate between these two at the start, when we are trying to bring our affections into order, and our hesitation can be a cause of disquiet. We feel that we do not sufficiently love what should be greatly loved, and that we have too much affection for what should be loved less. The right ordering of love demands that we love only what God wants us to love; that we love things in the degree that God wills them to be loved. If two things are to be loved in the same degree, we should love them equally. If one thing is to be loved more than another, we should not love it less than the other.

Let us imagine two different men. One has great virtues and does good to all men, but his look is severe and forbidding, and people do not find him attractive. The other is by contrast very attractive, full of gentleness and charm. He may not be as virtuous as the other man, but he is a good man for all that. We find no difficulty in loving him because our natural inclination is attracted to him. But it is not so for the more austere and more virtuous man. To love him, reason must dictate to our inclinations, and charity must be first set in order in us. And as long as we find ourselves less attracted to the better man, we cannot help feeling that something is wrong. We realize that we are loving one less and the other more than he deserves.

19

Two more comparisons on the same subject

THIS is where I must examine my own conscience, for I should hate to be deceived by my inclinations, which could be the case if I were ignorant of their origin. Let us begin then by saying that as long as the attractive personality of which we are speaking is that of a virtuous man, and not a man of evil life, our attraction to him must originate in virtue. It is therefore a good attraction, and it makes him an acceptable companion. But when we say that this attraction originates in virtue, why then are we not similarly moved towards the man who, while attracting us less, is evidently the more virtuous of the two? Perhaps this very fact implies that our more spontaneous inclination is really something carnal, and brought about by appearance alone. Yet if it were, we would be equally attracted to pleasant looking people whom we knew to be vicious in their lives. And to these we are decidedly not attracted to anything like the same degree. It has occasionally happened to me that I met someone who seemed very pleasant, and who gave me every reason to suppose that he was a good man. And I have found myself attracted to him until the moment when I discovered that his life was altogether different from what I had expected. Then all the attraction would disappear, leaving only revulsion.

From this we can conclude that the outward appearance of a man, whether he seems kindly or forbidding, is merely a container for what he possesses in his soul. The polished gentleman or the coarse peasant are all that we see from without. But the matter contained in a man, whether it be good or bad, virtuous or evil, is as it were the food of our souls, either good or bad for us, and thus our souls react to it. The fact is that the good food may often be kept in a poor looking container, and a vessel which appears to be of great value may be full of poison. When we know them better we do indeed find that virtue in the humble vessel pleases more, and vice nobly decked out fills us with disgust.

Still it remains true, as we said at the beginning of this chapter, that a lesser quantity of virtue in an attractive man appeals to us more than a greater virtue in a less attractive person. And here we may adopt another parallel, by comparing virtue with truth, and vice with falsehood. The forbidding aspect of our good man is like the rough speech of peasants, let us say, and the attractive appearance of the other man is like the conversation of cultivated people. But just as in pleasing words we cannot abide the presence of falsehood, likewise in the words which peasants use we never despise truth. In like manner, the virtues of our unattractive person still please us as virtues, and a man who appeals to us does not attract us to himself by means of evil living.

Until we know that a man is speaking the truth, it may well be that we are inclined more readily to believe someone who puts his case in a pleasant but pointed and purposeful manner, rather than someone who is blunt or awkward or just diffident. It is a real pleasure to listen to someone who knows how to stimulate an interest in people whose interest is normally difficult to arouse; someone who can reconcile others to his own point of view, and dispose everyone kindly towards himself with his opening remarks, arousing a pleasant anticipation that what he says will be worth hearing. Yet this man may be no more or no less honest than the orator whose manner is not so gracious. He simply has the gift of making the truth pleasant, doing us good in a manner we enjoy; whereas the other man gives a slightly acid flavour to the truth he propounds.

Now the more the truth pleases us by being made attractive, the more good it is bound to do us. Both men speak the truth. One may speak it more profoundly but less attractively; the other less profoundly but more pleasantly. And so the latter will please us most. We have then to make an effort not to be put off by the less attractive manner of the one who is offering us something more valuable. We may meet two men of a very different sort—the one kind, pleasant, attractive, cheerful and ingratiating; the other hard, austere, almost frighteningly serious. As long as we know no more about them than their appearance tells, as long as we are ignorant of their good and bad qualities, how are we to make a judgement on them if we let our feelings take the one to our hearts on the spot, and unreasonably reject the other outright? We may know them to be equal in virtue, or the pleasanter one to be less virtuous than the other, but still it is not surprising or unreasonable if truth is judged more pleasant when found in pleasant words, than virtue when found in much austerity of manners, which as we said was like truth in the speech of peasants. We take to the latter by having somewhat to force our wills. Each age of man has a certain manner of behaviour proper to it, and the speech that befits an old man is not the same as that which one anticipates in a younger person. In an older man, gaiety and animation tend to look odd, while in a younger man we take them for granted. But if in a younger man we find cheerfulness, kindness, consideration and readiness to be of service to others, and in an old man maturity and composure—why, then, we need never reproach the one for being light-minded or the other for being too severe.

However it may vary, our love towards these two will never violate the rule of charity if we do all that reason tells us to do, in the one case by not being excessively loving to the one who most attracts us, and in the other case by making an effort to be more loving than we feel to the one who pleases us less. Feelings, after all, are not entirely ours to command. We are attracted towards some against our will, while towards others we can never experience a spontaneous affection. If we are moved solely by our feelings, that is not love. Real love means that we are still master of our acts, and we use our inclinations and attractions simply as guides in the direction which we choose to take. And the same is true when reason tells us what direction love must take. It is not reason which impels us to love, it is we ourselves who choose to love, taking reason as our guide.

Love, then, takes its rise from feeling when we agree to let feeling guide us. It takes its rise from reason when our will consents to take reason as its guide. But a third love comes about when these three—reason, feeling and will—collaborate. The love that comes about through feeling is pleasant but it can be dangerous. It comes about through the experience of a pleasant attraction. The second, or reasonable one, is harder to achieve, but more fruitful. Reason compels the choice. The third is the best, and it has the full savour of real love. Love that is induced by mere feeling may well be good, but what we love in this way we love because it is pleasant, and nothing more. But in the full and perfect love which I placed last, we love not because it is pleasant to do so, but because it is the love of something worthy. Therefore it has its own sweetness and delight.

20

How to recognize the true love of God

FROM all that has been said, we can gather the main points about the chief constituents of love. First of all, if we choose something for our enjoyment, desire it inwardly, and outwardly pursue it by our actions so as to obtain it, that is love, without any doubt. And the more intensely we go about achieving what we desire, the more we can be presumed to love. If we are genuinely attracted to what we seek, we shall strive with so much the more ease, and love with so much the greater pleasure. If, however, it is reason that prompts us to act, we shall enjoy the pursuit of the beloved object less, but we shall get it none the less speedily. If our choice is a bad one, and we select something for our enjoyment which we should not, our enjoyment will likewise not be good. This is the perverse love which is the contrary of charity, namely greed. And as we said before, we are exceeding the measure of real love if we choose something other than God, or our neighbour in God, for our enjoyment.

Choice can be good even though the acts are bad whereby we go about achieving what we choose. For instance, if we choose to enjoy God, this choice is wise and good; but if we put our desire in carnal things, like the Jews, who supposed that heaven would be all feasting and pleasure, then our choice would be of no profit to us. And supposing we were to choose God and desire nought but Him, and yet proposed to get to heaven by squandering all our activity in ceremonies like those of the Jews, or in sacrifices like those of the pagans, our love would bear no fruit.

But if our choice is wise and our desire adequate to the end in view, and our behaviour reasonable in seeking what we love, then we do not go beyond the bounds of charity. It is moreover important that love should be pleasant, prudent and persevering, so that there be enjoyment from the first, with moderation and strength to overcome temptations on the way. If love is a pleasant experience there will be a true enjoyment of what we desire, and other attractions will be minimized, if they are noticed at all. If love is prudent there will be nothing unwise, mistaken or indiscreet in our behaviour, and if strong and persevering, it will not be overcome by any temptation or contrariety. When our love fulfils all these requirements it will be perfect indeed, full of joy and delight. But even if love should be without any great delight, we can still see to it that it is prudent and strong. And if it should bring no great joy in this life, it will surely reward us with joy in the life to come.

21

Some points concerning the love of our fellow men

IF, in the love of our fellow men, we are guided by our choice of their company as something that brings us nearer to God, then we have chosen well. If, on the other hand, our love is followed by impure desires and conduct, this will spoil everything that was originally good in our choice. When we love God we do so for our own benefit, not God's. He stands in no need of anything we might do for Him. But when we love each other, we have some regard for our mutual benefit. Our desires and actions in this case must have a twofold purpose. We must seek to enjoy one another in God, and at the same time to enjoy God in each other. Man is made up of body and soul, and our actions must be performed in regard to these two; and the more prudently and fervently we act, the more complete our charity will be. The more we love with our heart's inclination, the more delightful charity will be for us. To bring this about, as we said, reason must often command our inclinations. And now we must see which of our feelings we are to follow, and to what degree.

There are three inclinations which must be absolutely rejected. These are the spiritual inclination which comes from the devil, the one which is carnal, and the one which is unreasonable. All three are closely connected with vicious conduct. As far as we may, we must uproot these three from our hearts. But the spiritual inclination that comes from God is not only to be allowed, but actively encouraged and increased. It is the best guide for our desires, and the more we realize its great excellence and delight, the more we shall find it desirable, and long to have it always in our hearts. But as for ordering our acts as well, this is more than we can allow. We cannot let inclination do more than encourage our acts. It is a useful agent for helping the will not to slacken in well-doing. But as far as actually ordering our actions, this would be unwise since it could exceed the bonds of the body's capabilities. The body is an instrument which we use, and since it is of the earth earthly, subject to passions without number, it cannot stand up to the requirements of a zealous spirit unless its actions are prudently regulated. Our inclinations indeed often know no bounds; ignoring our body's strength and becoming involved in the body's passions, they may rush blindly to a beloved object, thinking only of what they seek, and unconscious of all else. Whatever is difficult or even impossible is undertaken as if no effort were required at all. Desire and pleasure can be so intense that outward labour goes unfelt. Here reason has a most necessary part to play, and if necessary it must be forced to rule over a will so influenced by desire that the body is driven beyond what it can tolerate. Instead of attaining sanctity through our desires, we can, without reason's help, only find exhaustion, for immoderate action can overcome inclination and discourage the will altogether.

22

Reasonable inclinations

REASONABLE inclinations are those which arise from the contemplation of another's virtues; these are the best means we have for increasing our love towards our fellow men. The love of virtue in others is indeed a good indication that we have some little virtue in ourselves. To follow this good inclination is most beneficial to us, either by imitating the virtues of others or by an abhorrence of the contrary bad acts which the goodness of others makes us hate more intensely. I would say that our desires, if directed according to this inclination, can never be bad. It is always good for us to desire to correct ourselves by means of good example, if we are not ourselves good. If we are already good, then good example can further our progress. And if we are as good as those whose goodness we admire, our love of goodness is strengthened the more. It is good to seek the company of the saints in this life, and even more to enjoy the presence of Christ in heaven for all eternity. We go on pilgrimage to the saints' shrines, but we go to Christ by living a holy and righteous life. We may follow our desire to lead a Christ-like life without hesitation, for inner holiness need fear no excess. But as for the actual exercise of virtues that we see practised in saints' lives, there we must be careful not to be too righteous.[51] Reason must be the moderator. The bodily presence of the saints is a useful thing for us to wish for, but we do not always need to seek for it, and here reason is our guide. How pleasant it was for the Christians of Antioch to have Paul and Barnabas with them, to instruct them, to give them good example, and to defend their faith from false teachers. Yet when they heard the voice of the Holy Spirit saying: *Separate to me Saul and Barnabas, for the work whereunto I have taken them,*[52] although this was against their inclination they laid hands on them and with a prayer dismissed them. And did not Paul prove Timothy's love by those tears his follower shed? Now if Timothy had followed his inclination, he would have followed Paul, but unreasonably.[53]

23

Friendship, based on mutual good offices

FRIENDSHIP is the most potentially dangerous of all our affections. It is good and useful but it must be used with care. What is more consonant with reason, what more worthy, than to repay the kindness done to us by our friends who love us; to be grateful to those who make us presents and to do services and favours to those who ask them of us? And what is more to be guarded against than encouraging evil men in their wrong doing, or being taken in by their servility? I am not speaking of those who love presents, seek acknowledgements and the payment of obligations, and who, having a venal idea of justice, are less fond of the giver than of his gifts. I am thinking now of those who, being touched by the kindnesses and gifts of others, are gratefully fond of the givers. Friendship means that we must never be ungrateful for a service rendered. But we must always be careful to keep the *man* in mind, rather than his gift. We must be moved to love the one who gives us good gifts, and to consider the person as such, so that if he merits it we may love him with a higher love, namely 'reasonable' love, on account of his virtues. It may well happen that the austere and unwelcoming sort of man of whom we have already spoken, may do us some good turn, and this will make such a difference to our estimation of him that we shall find that we are suddenly really attracted to him.

Virtue, which before we had merely accepted in him, we shall begin to enjoy as it deserves to be enjoyed. And if the man who does us a kindness be someone who does not show us any such virtue, friendship may uncover his virtues to us.

24

The love of kindred

IT is impossible for us not to have this inclination in us, and yet at the same time we are told: *If any man come to Me and hate not his father and mother, and his own life also, he cannot be My disciple.*[54] Therefore it must be a virtuous thing not to follow this inclination. But at the same time: *If any man have not care of his own, and especially of those of his house, he has denied the faith and is worse than an infidel.*[55] What are we to think of this? Are we to suppose that the disciple disagrees with the Master? Obviously not! We must therefore make the same distinction as before between our two loves—one of which follows our inclinations and the other one being guided by reason. It is natural for us to be kindly inclined to ourselves and our families, but we must not let this feeling rule our love, either towards ourselves or our kindred. It is reason which must rule our love. *No man ever hated his own flesh;*[56] this is because of natural human inclination. But Christ says that we cannot follow Him without hating our family and our life, meaning that our love must not be ruled solely by inclination. We must have a care for our own, so as not to become worse than the infidels, but at the same time we must not allow our affection to be exclusively bound up in our own. *Men shall be lovers of themselves,*[57] St. Paul says, and condemns such a love as he speaks of evils yet to come. This love always persuades us to do what is most easy and pleasant, making us *covetous, haughty, proud ... lovers of pleasure more than of God.*[58] Whatever is hard and difficult and against the will is avoided with horror. To follow this inclination gives us perverse love. A man turns into a beast, and whatever is good and worthy he buries out of sight. It is a love that is to be expected in animals who have no reason, and may be excused in children, whose use of reason is still undeveloped. Whoever loves his life shall lose it, our Saviour tells us, and he who hates his life in this world will fight to keep it for all eternity. Saint Augustine tells us that if we love badly we are really hating, whereas if we hate well, then we are really loving.[59] If we love according to mere inclination, then we are hating our own souls. But if we hate according to our inclinations, we are loving in a way that is reasonable, for in the world the things we hate are concupiscence of the flesh and of the eyes, and the pride of life.[60] If we love our souls in the sense of following our carnal inclinations, it means that we love them in this life with concupiscence and pride, for these are the things towards which carnal appetite inclines us.

The distinction gives an answer to a question which sometimes occurs, namely what difference is there between our love for God and our love of each other for God's sake? An inclination is not something we assume for the love of God. It simply happens in the soul. Now if this inclination goes out spontaneously to someone, all our love goes with it, guided by that inclination. That person is loved neither in God, nor for God's sake, but rather for his own sake. If, on the other hand, we love someone according to our inclinations and love him for God's sake as well, the reason is playing its part. Here we have a love which is not primarily activated by the love of God, but it is certainly a love of which God approves. Now supposing that there is someone to whom we feel no attraction whatever, but to whom we show all the consideration he requires, and all the affection we can muster, then we are loving someone exclusively for God's sake. A friend cannot but be loved. Therefore we must take care to love him in God. But someone towards whom we can feel no attraction, whom we cannot love for his own sake, is loved for God's sake alone. When we love our friends, we do so according to our inclination. But toward those to whom we are not attracted as friends, reason is our guide.

This is how due moderation is kept in the love of kindred. We are meant to love, and to feel the warmth of love, but in all things reason must have the last word. Joseph showed his love for his brethren by the tears he wept. If he had allowed reason to hold back those tears, his brothers would not have had the chance to ask pardon for their conduct towards him. Our Lord, likewise, wept over Jerusalem, but this did not prevent Him from punishing the city which had earned destruction through the evil ways of its people. If only those who rule the Church could do the same. Do we not find bishops and even abbots whose houses give us an impression of Sodom and Gomorrha when we go in? There they have about them a host of young relatives, whose vices they make no attempt to correct, in no wise drawing them away from worldly vanity and pleasure, but even indulging their depraved tastes and paying for them with the price of Christ's blood. They, as Joel said, have put their sons in a brothel,[61] encouraging them in effeminate ways, and having them grow their hair long and dress in clothes that reveal the body shamelessly. Among these Thy Sacrifice, O Christ, is offered, and Thy Cross they raise up, and all the while they see Thy wounds, yet scorn Thy scourging and crucify Thee afresh in the poor whom they oppress, as they go about hawking and hunting on hard-driven horses. Thou must see it, dear Lord, yet Thou art silent. Wilt Thou ever be silent? No, surely Thou must speak some day!

Physical attraction

THIS is an attraction which is brought about by external appearance. We must not shun it as if it were evil, nor must we allow ourselves to be too much drawn to it. It is near to the inclination that leads to vice, and unless we are on our guard against the latter, we can be carried away by it. But as long as we find virtue among the attractions which appeal to us in anyone's outward appearance, and as long as we allow ourselves to be drawn by it moderately and sensibly, then we have nothing to fear. But if we sense anything vicious in what we see in others, we must be determined not to let ourselves be attracted. What we have said in regard to the attraction of friendship, applies here. But whoever finds he is in any way still attracted by the sins of the flesh, let him take great heed in regard to the physical attractions of others, for he will almost always find there is something dangerous in them.

26

The origin and development of attractions

IN some mysterious way, an attraction we feel towards others will sometimes turn imperceptibly into something else. Let us take for instance the case of someone who hears of some holy nun who has gained great repute. Her fame has become widely known because of her evident sanctity, her faith, her wisdom, her absolute obedience and renunciation of the world. It is most reasonable that we should admire such virtue, and this is indeed precisely what we have already called a 'reasonable' love. But let us suppose that someone has gone to ascertain her holiness for himself, and being much taken by it begins not only to enjoy her conversation and company, but will speak much in her praise to others and will write to her and give her little presents. Reasonable love can thus develop little by little into friendship, with all the usual obligations and acknowledgements. And this friendship can in time change into something really dangerous, if it becomes familiar and tender and sought after for its own sake.

I myself have known good and holy men who have had an extreme horror of anything unclean, being most chaste and continent, yet they have fallen in love with young nuns to whom they had originally been attracted because of their virtues. These young women had progressed to a great spiritual maturity, and friendship grew and became so irresistibly delectable that evil somehow managed to work its way into pure affection, causing much sorrow.

Friendship can easily degenerate, unfortunately, into carnal lust. A pure heart may yet embrace some impure object, or what seems to be purity and goodness in someone who is in fact not as pure or as good as he or she might seem. Our love of others, albeit reasonable or even spiritual, must be well under control before we can indulge it in the direction of persons who might be dangerous on account of their age or their sex. Endearments and tokens of love must not be indulged in, unless we really know what we are doing, and do it with moderation and prudence, in order that the virtues we love and praise in others may be the more encouraged.

The priority of inclinations

THESE various conflicting feelings in the soul raise the problem of how they shall be properly ordered and organized. We must consider which is to be preferred to another, and how the better may be given place over what is less good. We can think of the struggle in Abraham's soul when he was ordered to sacrifice his only son Isaac, for whom he naturally felt all a father's love, while at the same time the love of God had to come uppermost. Jonathan too, instead of acquiescing to his own father's plan to kill David, followed the dictates of reasonable love for his virtuous friend. Nor is it any wonder that his love for his friend was greater than that he bore towards his father. And when David fled from Saul into hiding, Jonathan came to him to tell him of his father's plans, showing his love by embraces and tears. *Thou wilt be king and I will be second after thee,*[62] he said, for he was innocent of greed and envy, putting his friend before his own kingdom. *I will be second after thee,* he said, renouncing what was his own by right of inheritance. He preferred to serve under David rather than take to himself all the honours that would belong to him as king. When would one find even a blood brother doing such a thing as this? Who else would have given up all his own hopes in favour of his friend? The sons of Jacob,[63] envying Joseph the favourite, sent their own brother into slavery and inflicted the deepest grief on their father. Aaron barely escaped the wrath of God through the prayers of Moses, the meek brother he envied.[64] Solomon too, wisest of men, was not innocent of envy towards his brother.[65] Only Jonathan, do we read, put his father, the king, and the country of his inheritance at less value than his great friend David. He could rightly have said: 'I will be king and thou shalt be second after me'. If he had done this it would have been no violation of the laws of friendship.

They both wept, but David, we are told, wept most.[66] They were about to be separated and their separation they felt to be more bitter than death, since it would be the end of all their mutual exchange of confidences, their consolation in all troubles. Jonathan was bound to his father by a son's obligations, but to David he was bound by feelings of love and friendship. His duty was to look after his father in old age, and if he were to cleave to David, he would be ignoring his duty to his father. Yet he owed a friend's love to David and his pledge could not be broken.

Therefore, although their love urged them to stay together, reason bade them separate. They paid the debt of friendship with their tears, and being forced to part, did so in obedience to reason. Each wept, because he loved. But why did David weep more bitterly? Jonathan had already predicted that David would inherit the kingdom, while he, Jonathan, took second place. The law of friendship ordained, then, that these injured friends should have the consolation of compassionate tears. David, in later years, wept for the son who met his end as a would-be parricide, because of his most natural affection for that son.[67] But he accepted the reproach of a soldier and left his private grief to go and rejoice with the victorious army. And Our Lord himself, naturally enough, asked His Father that the chalice might be taken from Him—yet His reason added, *not as I will....*[68] Thus, in all our inclinations this rule must be followed, namely that the feeling that most encourages us to the love of God is most to be esteemed and placed above the others. First in this order comes the love guided by reason, then the love of friendship, then the love of kindred. By distinguishing these various sorts of love, we can see that their chief usefulness is in stimulating us to action. The more love we feel, the more delight and fervour we shall find in going in search of the object of our love. Desire excites love, and, as we have already seen, it must go before love to show the way. It must not be dragged willy nilly after. Love incites us to good works, and to do good works lovingly is a very good thing. But these must not be regulated by love alone, for that would be unreasonable.

28

Action towards God and our fellow men

THERE are some actions which we perform in order that we may spiritually reach God, who is our highest good, and the one who is most supremely to be loved. There are others which we do because they are necessary either for ourselves or for our neighbour, either for bodily benefit or salvation of soul, and these two are ultimately referred to God as to their end. In Saint Paul's words, we must lead a sober, just and pious life in this world[69] and in this one sentence, the perfection of life on this earth is contained. By sobriety we understand temperance and due proportion, the prudent avoidance of excess being the happy medium between extremes. Wise philosophers have called this virtue 'frugality' and some have even considered it the very greatest of virtues. In God, our highest good, there is no possibility of default or excess, and this is the measure we must take for our model, for when we are joined to Him in eternity, the same will be true for us—we shall desire nothing more than we already possess in Him, and nothing of all that great possession will be too much for us. The proportion we must strive after in this life implies the avoidance of any lack which may enfeeble us, and of any extravagance which may fill us with pride.

The justice of which Paul speaks in this maxim is, I think,

the virtue which causes us to consider the need, either bodily or spiritual, of our fellow men. We must give to each according to his need, putting the most needy first, and remembering always the due priority of greater and more necessary gifts over smaller and less necessary ones. And the reason why piety must be joined to sobriety and justice is that we could be tempted, without it, to be puffed up with pride in our holy manner of life, like the pagan philosophers. Piety means pure intentions and sincere faith. We have already considered the importance of choice in selecting what we wish to love, and this is where intention is important. Here perhaps the reader might wish me to consider in more detail the difficulties and dangers involved in exceeding the due proportion laid down in Saint Paul's words, but this, as he will see, is a very difficult thing to do. How can one lay down any general rule when there are so many different sorts of men to consider, so many different qualities involved in considering each individual? How rarely does one find two people alike, two people for whom the same quantity is sufficient? You are much more likely to find that what you consider sufficient for any two men is too much for one and too little for the other! One man's meat may well be another man's poison. All we can lay down, then, as a general rule is what may or may not apply to all, and so each one of you must use his own common sense, and apply the rule according to his needs.

29

Three ways of life

WE may consider three ways of life. There is the one into which we are born, and which we are most bound to follow since it belongs to our nature. Secondly there is the manner of life by means of which we make reparation for the abuse of what is allowed us in our natural way of life, by restraining our appetites and abstaining from what is licit. Finally there is the monastic life, which we take up of our own free will, without any obligation.

The things which God allows us in this life are all pure to the pure, and none of them is to be rejected. All are to be accepted with gratitude.[70] These are things like the use of marriage, eating meat, drinking wine, possessing wealth. This is all part of the natural order of human life, using things that are lawful for us, in the lawful way God expects of us. God has granted us these things as free gifts. They are in our power to use in the way that He pleases, and we would be heretics if we, like those of whom Paul speaks, were to forbid marriage and abstain from meats which God has created to be received with thanksgiving by the faithful.[71] But to make the use of these things licit, we have to consider circumstances of time and place, and varying modes of life. Moderation is to be observed in everything, and excess is always a fault, as Our Lord implies when He charges us to avoid surfeiting and drunkenness and being too much involved in the cares of this life.[72] Paul, speaking of matrimony, bids us know how to possess each his vessel in sanctification and honour, and not in the passion of lust.[73] When he speaks of the body's clothing he shows that he disapproves of costly attire.[74] Thus, in the use of things licit, there is still need for some measure of temperance. Our food and drink must not be of such a quantity that we fall into drunkenness and gluttony, and our clothes must be worn for necessity, and not for mere ornament. If we possess riches we must guard against caring about them too much. If we are married, we must not be led by shameful lusts. We must remember that there is a proper time for everything, as for instance on the fast days of the church it would be wrong to break the fast without good reason, and at times more specially dedicated to prayer it would not be right for married people to have intercourse. On feast days, when we are bound to hear the Word of God preached, we must not spend the time instead in daily business. In the solemn seasons of penance, we do not deck ourselves out in all our finery. In fact, we must always remember where we are, and what season we are in. Anyone who conducted business in church or had sexual intercourse there, would be judged guilty of sacrilege. Paul accused the Corinthians of not taking their food and drink at the right time when he wrote: *When you come therefore together into one place, it is not now to eat the Lord's supper, for everyone takes before his own supper to eat.*[75] Instead of observing the proper time, they ate the common food before taking the Eucharist, which was against the tradition they had received from Paul. And so one would be hungry and another one drunk. Had they not houses to eat and to drink in? he asked, and did they then despise the church of God?[76]

Saint Paul also considered whether or not Christians could be allowed to eat meats that had been offered to idols, without sacrilege.[77] The use of such things, as also of things which have been stolen and obtained in some other dishonest way, is forbidden when he says: *If any man say: This has been sacrificed to idols, do not eat of it.*[78] Tobias, likewise, when he heard the young kid bleating that had been given to his wife Anna as payment for her weaving work, said: *Take heed, lest perhaps it be stolen.*[79] He feared that some injustice was being done to another man, and that he would thereby incur a fault himself. These are just some of the cases we have to bear in mind in respect of the normal ordering of our lives. There are many other cases which we might also have included, but these any sensible man may think out for himself. Now we will go on to consider what I call the 'order of necessity' as opposed to the basic order of nature.

30

Satisfaction for sin

THE necessity of which we now have to speak is this, namely that when we have abused those things which we are allowed to use in the normal course of life, we must make satisfaction by refraining, in some degree, from their use. And in the restrictions we place on these things, we must bear in mind firstly the means of making satisfaction, and secondly the need of making this satisfaction for the benefit of our soul. The means is important because it must correspond in gravity to the offence committed. As Saint John the Baptist says, we must bring forth worthy fruits of penance.[80] The exact degree of satisfaction I leave of course to the holy doctors and fathers of the church who have extensively written about it. I for my part have nothing to add to what they have said on the subject. But we will consider for the moment our need of making satisfaction, for our soul's benefit and its purification from sin. We must restrain ourselves from the use of what is licit, not only to make satisfaction to God for our past sins, but in order to diminish and quieten our passions, and this requires much patient effort, for evil habit may have made the passions strong. The outward exercise of virtue is an instrument for the soul, cutting away vicious habit, and cleansing the heart.

Therefore it behoves us first to find out what are the passions which chiefly trouble us, and to decide what are the best means for fighting them. By careful consideration we can find a weapon wherewith to fight each thing inimical to our souls, putting particular energy into fighting the ones which have the most power over us. And we shall find no doubt that the best weapon to fight lust with is fasting, and vigils the best corrective to a light and wandering temperament. Silence is your sword against anger. In every case, bad acts are countered by an effort of the soul. We must always remember of course not to let an excessive preoccupation with one virtue countering one vice weaken us for the practice of other virtues against other vices. Too much concentration on one fault may blind us to the fact that we have others, which also need to be dealt with. And I think this is enough for the moment about the fight against evil inclinations. Cassian has dealt with the subject at great length, and I can refer you to him for a much more developed treatment, in his book of *Institutions* for those who have renounced the world and its pleasures.

31

Voluntary sacrifice

I will freely sacrifice to Thee,[81] says the psalmist to his Lord, and it is this life of free sacrifice of which we are now about to speak. The monastic life is a sacrifice which we make of our own free will, and it is a sacrifice which God welcomes, for it is pleasing in His sight. We leave behind us the use of what is allowed in normal life, to follow the precepts of Our Lord in the Gospel, striving with a willing heart for a prize which promises greater glory. If we would be perfect, Our Saviour tells us, we must go and sell all that we have and give it to the poor,[82] so that we may thereafter follow Him. There are some, He says, who have made themselves eunuchs for the kingdom of heaven,[83] and for those to whom Our Lord's meaning is clear, these words must be taken to heart. To lead a life of complete chastity, to give up the world, to take on a more austere way of life— these are sacrifices freely made. And what is more, when we have given up the world, we cannot go back to it, just

128

as we cannot indulge in any carnal pleasure once we have taken a vow of chastity. Once we have taken on the hard life of the monastery, our salvation is in peril if we leave it. This does not, of course, make the willing sacrifice a matter of coercion, since in the first place no one is forced to take on the austere life. But it makes it imperative that, before deciding we will take the hard road, we think over what we are doing, and what we propose to do. We must consider all that the monastic life involves, and whether we have sufficient physical strength to stand up to the rigours of manual labour, and sufficient inner strength to withstand the daily assaults of temptation. There is of course bound to be plenty of labour, both for body and soul, in any state of life, but there is a special need for the mortifying labours of the body where the filth of the passions needs to be washed away, whereas the spiritual side of our endeavour is like a sweet perfume pervading all our works. Such a sweetness and unction are not to be expected in the man who is under the sway of passions; his principal need is for bodily mortification. When, however, the passions are brought under control and cause us less trouble, then we can refrain somewhat from severe bodily penance, and concentrate more on our prayers. But this we must be careful not to do in any way that goes beyond what our rule of life lays down, for there is a time and a place for everything in the rule, and we must follow it faithfully. We must spend whatever time we are bidden on each work as it comes, and we can then exercise ourselves in each, either more fervently or with some relaxation, according to our need.[84]

32

The due proportion to be observed in the consecrated life

WE who seek after the heights of perfection by giving our will to God in a life dedicated to the pursuit of holiness, must, above all, keep charity in our mind's eye as the goal of our endeavour. Charity draws us to God. Charity makes us cleave to God by conforming us to Him. In charity all the fullness of perfection is contained. It is the end towards which we strive, and to which all our life must be directed. And with this aim always in mind, we must travel the road laid down for us by our rule or profession, with a good heart. The things that help us on our way are abstinence, vigils, meditating on God's word, and working with our hands. And if any of these helps is omitted or dispensed, doing damage instead of good service to charity, then the one who is allowed to make dispensations must so arrange things that charity be not made to suffer because of the dispensations he allows. All concerned must be reminded that charity comes first. The superior must see to it that only extreme necessity is allowed as an excuse for setting aside what the rule lays down. Otherwise dispensation becomes something more like destruction. At certain times, certain points of the rule may be modified, according to the needs of everyone's state of health, bodily or spiritual. This is exactly what Saint Benedict says in respect of manual labour. 'Let him (the abbot) order and arrange things with the salvation of his monks' souls in mind. Whatever the brethren do must be done without grumbling.[85] Let everything be done in moderation, for the sake of the weaker brethren.'[86] He does not say that anything is to be totally neglected or set aside on their account. Far from it; he stipulates, in fact, that not even the sick and feeble should be left in idleness, even though they are exempt from heavy work. They are to be given some work that they are capable of doing.[87] No one is entirely exempt from work. The due measure to be observed here is that any one point that raises a particular difficulty is to be dispensed so that all the other points may be better safeguarded, and the point in which anyone thus dispensed most excels can be concentrated on with particular vigour.

In the realm of human conduct we have to consider what is due from us, whether from precept, or on account of what we have freely vowed. First of all we must do the things which are meritorious if done and if left undone must condemn us. This means that the things we must put first are those which it is sinful not to do. After these, if we have added anything as a work of supererogation, we must do it so that our due service be not impeded in any way. Some make a supererogation of things they need not do, because they cannot do the things they should do. But there are those who, even though they could do what God expects of them, adduce impediments of their own free will, making supererogation of things they need not do instead.

Finally, two bad things are to be guarded against in the good acts we do. When our activity becomes a burden, all enjoyment goes and we become bitter and dissatisfied, and when we are too much involved in our occupations, we lose our peace of mind. We must therefore guard against impatience at not being able to do all we would like to do, and also doing too much of the things we like doing. We must put up with our inability patiently, and be moderate when we are tempted to go beyond what is reasonable.

33

Duty towards self, and duty towards one's fellow men

WE have spoken of the due measure to be observed in various situations of life, and these situations are, after all, only so many steps whereby we rise up to the One who is to be loved above all else. And as we climb up towards the contemplation of God, we are at the same time looking after the salvation of our souls and taking that care of our bodies which they need. Since God has taught us that we must love our fellow men and ourselves, it is first of all necessary that we should know how to go about obeying these two commandments. Then we have to see to it that we put the commandment into effect without sinning by excess on one side or the other. In this connection, it is obvious that in any society there are three categories to be considered, namely those who command, those who obey, and those who live together in obedience to each other. And if the due measure is not observed in our society, then it behoves the superiors, when necessary, to enforce God's will. Those who live together must correct each other. And if it is those in command who offend, then it belongs to their subjects to point out where they have failed. But it must always be remembered that those who enforce the law must do so with compassion, just as those who point out a fault to someone in authority over them must show respect while doing so. And when we correct each other we must always be motivated by fellow feeling. Whoever shows himself to belong rightly in a humbler state, can be advised, but not forced, to move up. Whoever leaves a more exalted state of his own free will must be treated according to the state he has accepted. He must not be made to undertake a more rigorous way than the one he has already willingly taken on. Likewise we must be careful in the matter of loving our fellow men, for we must indeed love them as we love ourselves. We must not love ourselves too much, and neglect the One whom we must love more than all others.

Now there are some who would claim that loving our neighbour as ourselves,[88] means that we are to love the generality of men as we love ourselves, but that we may love one or two special friends more than ourselves. This means in effect that they love their own damnation. What indeed can a man give in exchange for his own soul? What is it to him that he gains the whole world (and even saves it from perdition) if he loses his own soul? Whatever good he may have done, according to all the laws laid down for charity that we have already seen, if he loses his own soul he offends against the love of God. The measure wherewith he loves God will be the measure of his love of himself. The less he loves God, the less he must love himself. But if he loves himself he spares many a man from perdition. How can he love others, who does not love himself? Saint Paul said that he chose to be anathema from Christ for the sake of his fellow Jews,[89] so that he might take them to Christ by means of his own immense love for Christ. He shows us his love in these words, but he obviously does not mean that he would wish to lose Christ. Reason and love can often, as we have seen, show diverse facets in one and the same human spirit. When Paul said he chose to be anathema from Christ for the sake of his brethren, he spoke truly, for he said what his heart felt. But his reason told him none the less that it were better to choose the destruction of the whole world rather than be separated from Christ. Our Lord Himself wished for the cup to pass from Him, and reasonably enough since no man hates his own flesh.[90] But His reason in fact chose to drink that cup.

The scriptures advisedly tell us not to love our neighbour as much as ourselves, but simply *as* ourselves.[91] It is a manner of love that we have to learn, not a degree of love that we have to acquire. Thus we must show ourselves first that we do indeed love ourselves as God commanded us. Firstly we must consider our soul, which is the most eminent part of us, and secondly the body and its needs. And if we have to choose between the two, we must see to it that the body rather than the soul suffers injury. But even this does not mean that we can despise our bodies. It simply means that we must put our souls first. We must never depart from this kind of love for ourselves, and we must always keep it well in mind, so that we may be the safer in our dealings with our fellow men. The same measure is to be observed with them, in that our care for them must consider firstly their souls and secondly their bodies. If either body or soul be neglected, then we are not loving them as they should be loved. If a man's soul cannot be saved without some bodily suffering, we must let things be as God wills, that his soul may be saved in God's good time. We for our part must pity him in his afflictions, and sorrow for him the while, but no reason on earth can justify our losing our souls for the sake of our brethren's salvation, nor must we do away with our bodies in order to save the lives of our fellow men. We are commanded to lay down our lives for our brethren,[92] and this means that we must count our lives as little for their sake, but not suffer any injury to our souls on their account.

To lay down one's life, not for perdition but for salvation, redounds to the good of one's soul. Vassals, who protect the lives of their masters in battle by dying for them, do so for their own souls and not merely for the lives of their masters, if they do so for the sake of proving their loyalty. If they do so for mere renown, and to avoid the shame of disloyalty, they are laying down their lives for a foolish reason, yet this may be praiseworthy if they do so for the sake of love. But if anyone suffers injury to his own soul, whether on behalf of another's soul, or even for the whole world's salvation, it would be against the dictates of true love. It is injury to our souls if we desert the love of God, who is to be loved above all others. If we do something worthy of damnation or leave undone something necessary for salvation, we are deserting God's love. But if the salvation of our brethren requires it, various things can be dispensed, or varied, or changed, even wholly set aside—as, for instance, meditation and reading, work, fasting, the consolation that comes with prayer, and so on. We have to seek not what is our own but what belongs to others.[93] Saint Paul said that he tried to please others in all things, not seeking what was good for himself but what was conducive to the salvation of all.[94] He chose to be anathema from Christ for the sake of his brethren, by which we understand that he would do without the intimacy of prayer with Jesus, the contemplation of His heavenly mysteries, the sweetness of compunction that pours through the soul. Instead of all these, he would take the world with all its confusion, if the salvation of his brethren called for it. For those who have had the experience of resting in the love of Christ, and have tasted the sweetness of His conversation, to take the world instead is separation and anathema from Christ indeed. But whoever is thus drawn away from Christ for the sake of the brethren must see to it that he does not entirely lose the sweetness of Christ's presence through the needs of the brethren. What we have said about dispensation in the matter of reading and prayer, we must likewise repeat in respect of the body and its needs. Whatever we think necessary to do for our own salvation, can be equally necessary for the salvation of others.

34

The spiritual meaning of Noah's Ark

WE have seen what charity lays down for us to do in regard to ourselves and our brethren, and since it is obvious that we cannot go to the help of all our fellow men, we must now consider the order that obtains in this regard. Let us imagine our heart to be a kind of spiritual Noah's Ark, made of the imperishable wood of virtues and good deeds. There we shall find various compartments on different levels made ready for the different kinds of people we shall meet. Just as Noah had to look after wild beasts,[95] we have to find room in our hearts for those who are out for our blood— our enemies, that is, who hate us. We can give them our prayers, and any temporal help we can, but only after we have seen to the needs of those more closely connected with us. Let us, then, leave the lower floor and the outbuildings for our enemies, and keep the inner rooms and the upper floors for those nearer to us. The animals which are not wild but are still none the less earthly and unclean (let us say domestic animals, and crawling things) come next. These are not carnal and bloodthirsty men, and they have nothing against us. Their needs come next, and they deserve our prayers, our encouragement, and occasionally our correction. Of these, some may be connected with us through ties of blood, or of gratitude, which give them a claim to our intimacy. On the top floor, where Noah lodged his family, we can put those who have nothing in common with the beasts, being neither given to anger nor lust nor uncleanness. They are typical men whose desires do not yet carry them higher than a human ideal of perfection. And among these, we must take to us more especially those who are near to us by family ties, or by friendship, or by deeds of kindness. The topmost floor of all being reserved to

Noah's birds, we must find a place there for those whom we know to be specially near to God, flying up to heaven, as it were, on wings of virtue, above the normal state of men. And here again, we shall find that there are some special few of this number who are more closely allied to us than others, those, that is, for whom we have a most special place in our hearts, whose companionship is particularly dear to us and whom we cherish more sweetly and embrace more ardently in our hearts. But above all these there is a place reserved for the one who is above even the highest of our acquaintances, and that is Jesus, Our Lord, who made the Noah's ark of our hearts in the first place, and repaired it after it had fallen in ruin. All that is beneath Him He gathers to Himself, and transfuses into all things His own sweet savour, His light and His splendour, drawing everything to His own love. He alone, in all these, above all these, takes all our love to Himself, demanding it for His use alone. He makes His dwelling over all else in our hearts, and in the very depths of our souls.

And so we can make room for everyone in our hearts if we arrange things in this manner, seeing to it that the greater is always preferred to the less, while the lesser is still properly cared for.

35

The enjoyment of friendship

ONLY one thing now remains for us to consider, and that is something that comes of the distinction we have just made. We have defined charity as the choice of what God desires us to choose, the attainment of the same in the way that God approves, and its use in the manner that God has ordained. We have spoken sufficiently of choice and of the means of achieving what we have chosen. But a question arises as to the use of what we love, which may still be anything but good, even though our choice, and the means we chose, were good. When we have attained the object of our desire, we may still make errors of judgement and of conduct. Can we—are we indeed able—to enjoy all men or even some of our brethren to the same degree? There is an enjoyment that belongs to this life of which Paul speaks when he prays that he may enjoy Philemon,[96] and an eternal one, our enjoyment of each other in heaven, like the enjoyment of the angels, which is purely spiritual. Enjoyment means using something with joy and delight, and I take it for granted that we cannot all enjoy each other. Our true enjoyment is bound to be restricted to a small number. Our relations with our enemies, for instance, can only benefit us as a trial of virtue. Our teachers and masters are there to instruct us, and we turn to our elders for comfort in sorrow. If we have any bodily need we approach those who can furnish us with what we ask. But only our friends, whom we love, can give us spiritual delight and the joys that make life sweeter. Our friends we can indeed use with joy and delight, even in this present life. Charity, then, must be shown by all, to all, in so far as we must all choose the good and try to achieve it. But as to enjoying goodness, then obviously no one can enjoy goodness in every man he meets. There are few indeed, if any, who are able to love all mankind with the heart's affection as well as the will's intent. There are many, too, whose love of God will bring no enjoyment in this life, and that is because this joy is reserved for them in the life to come. And even if we enjoy the light of contemplation and the sweetness of compunction which are certainly a foretaste of the delights that await us with God, when we consider the infinitely greater joys that will be ours in heaven, the consolations of this life are clearly not the full enjoyment of God; they are simply a benefit which God confers on us.

The sweetness of God that we taste in this life is given us, not so much for enjoyment as for a consolation and encouragement for our weakness. That is why it is such a great joy to have the consolation of someone's affection—someone to whom one is deeply united by the bonds of love; someone in whom our weary spirit may find rest, and to whom we may pour out our souls . . . someone whose conversation is as sweet as a song in the tedium of our daily life. He must be someone whose soul will be to us a refuge to creep into when the world is altogether too much for us; someone to whom we can confide all our thoughts. His spirit will give us the comforting kiss that heals all the sickness of our preoccupied hearts. He will weep with us when we are troubled, and rejoice with us when we are happy, and he will always be there to consult when we are in doubt. And we will be so deeply bound to him in our hearts that even when he is far away, we shall find him together with us in spirit, together and alone. The world will fall asleep all round you, you will find, and your soul will rest, embraced in absolute peace. Your two hearts will lie quiet together, united as if they were one, as the grace of the Holy Spirit flows over you both. In this life on earth we can love a few people in this way, with heart and mind together, for they are more bound to us by the ties of love than any others. Our Lord Jesus Christ is our example in this too, for we know that there was one whom He loved above all the rest. If anyone should look askance at such a love let him remember how Jesus came to take pity on us, transforming our love by showing us His. He showed us that love by giving His heart as a resting place for one head in particular. This was a special sign of love for the beloved disciple, given to one alone, not

to all. All were loved equally, no one doubts it, but for
Saint John He had a special love, as we can see by the name
he gives himself, 'the disciple whom Jesus loved'.[97]

36

Enjoying in the Lord

THEREFORE, whoever finds enjoyment in the love of a friend,
let him enjoy him in the Lord, and not after the fashion of
this world. Let his enjoyment be a spiritual delight, with
no hint in it of the pleasures of the flesh. But you may ask
me what I mean by 'enjoying in the Lord', in which case
I will quote Saint Paul: 'Jesus Christ . . . is made unto us
wisdom and justice and sanctification.'[98] Now since Our
Lord is wisdom, justice and sanctification, to enjoy someone
in the Lord means enjoying him in wisdom, justice and
sanctification. Wisdom dismisses from our friendship all
worldly vanity. Sanctification excludes anything sordid and
fleshly, while justice puts an end to flattery and adulation.
With these to safeguard it, charity can then be truly of a
pure heart, good conscience, and faith without deceit.[99] A
pure heart will take easily to wisdom. Modesty will ensure
a clear conscience, and true faith is an extra ornament for
justice. There are those who enjoy each other in stupid and
futile pursuits, in worldly show, extravagance and vanity.
Since they do not enjoy one another in wisdom, they cannot
enjoy one another in Our Lord, who is the wisdom of
God. Nor can they enjoy each other in sanctification, if
their pursuit of lust has already transformed them into
animals. Sanctification means the sweetness of chastity
among other things, and there is no chastity among those
who pursue the pleasures of the flesh and the satisfaction of
impure desires. And those who only enjoy each other for

the flattery they mutually exchange, never dare give offence to each other, and so are not even at liberty to enjoy each other in justice.

If we love our friends for the consolation of their company, let our conversation be about good and serious things; let us reflect on the problems of life, and the guidance we get from the scriptures in these matters. We can share the burdens of our daily lives, and the hope of our future happiness that makes us happy even now as we look forward to it together. We can share our secret thoughts and strive together in our longing for the sight of Jesus' face. And when we do take a rest from more serious pursuits (as indeed we must occasionally) even though our pastimes may not be particularly elevating, at least let there be nothing bad about them, nothing foolish. We must enjoy one another, remember, in sanctification, which means, as Saint Paul says, that we must remember that each of us possesses his vessel (his body, that is) in sanctification and honour, and not in the passion of desire. And our enjoyment must be in justice, so that we may exhort one another in a spirit of freedom. We need to correct one another at times, and must not forget that even if a friend's corrections make us smart, they are worth far more to us than all the false endearments of those who do not love us at all.[100]

COLOPHON

THIS is the end of my meditations on charity, dearest Father, and if there is anything of worth in them, any profit, any beauty of composition, let them be called, as you suggested, a 'Mirror of Charity': some little reflection of charity itself. I only beg you not to show it in public, in case anyone should see in the Mirror some horrid picture of the author, instead of the shining beauty of love. If, as I suspect, this happens to be the case, then I ask whoever reads my book to remember that I wrote it not because I was proud of my abilities, but because you asked me to write it. I felt obliged to write it because you are my father, and it is yours to command. At the same time you are my brother, and if I love you I must do as you wish. I had no wish to run the risk of disobeying my superior, and at the same time I enjoyed telling you all I thought about charity because it somehow brought you near to me. And for my own benefit, I must say I found it useful to gather my wandering thoughts into a single volume. If anyone should read it and gather from it any useful thoughts, or conceive by its help any desires profitable to his salvation, then my labours are paid. All I would ask is that whoever reads the book will say a prayer for me, that the great number of my sins be forgiven me.

APPENDIX

MOST of the MSS. of the *Speculum Charitatis* are prefaced by a letter of Saint Bernard, who writes: 'In Christ's name and by the Spirit of our God do I command you to write down without delay what your own meditations have taught you about the excellence of charity, the fruits of charity, and everything that charity involves. Thus, as in a mirror, others may come to understand what charity is, how its possession brings delight, and how its contrary vice, cupidity, imposes nothing but tyranny. Your book will show how false it is to think that charity is lessened by a life of austerity, and that in fact austerity increases charity. It will tell us also how charity must be exercised and manifested in our conduct. And because you feel so embarrassed about writing the book, you can put this letter of mine as a preface to it, so that if anyone is not pleased with what you have written in your *Mirror of Charity* (that is the title I wish the book to have), he can blame me, for having forced you to write against your will, instead of you, who did the work under obedience.'

Bernard's letter is followed by Aelred's reply in which he accepts the task. The three stipulations regarding the subjects the work should cover have been carefully complied with, as we can judge by the words: 'I have divided the whole work into three parts, although various themes will be found to run throughout the work. The first part aims to prove the excellence of charity from the fact of its own innate dignity, and from the baseness of cupidity which is its contrary vice. The second part provides answers to some stupid objections (against the monastic life) and the third explains how charity is to be manifested and exercised.' He adds, significantly: 'Lest the length of the work should daunt the reader's resolve, let him first glance through the chapter headings to see what he would prefer to read, and what he would rather leave out.'

There has been some controversy about who the instigator of

the *Speculum* really was, the problem arising in the first instance from a mistaken attribution of the prefatory letter to Abbot Gervaise of Louth Park. Dom Wilmart deals with the question in the *Revue d'Ascétique et de Mystique*, 1933, p. 329, and concludes that the attribution to Gervaise stems from a later, continental MSS. tradition. In the MSS. circulating in England (those of the normal edition, that is, produced at Rievaulx) the letter is uniformly attributed to Bernard of Clairvaux. If it seems strange that Bernard should have ordered Aelred to write his *Speculum* direct, without sending his request through the superior of Rievaulx, we must remember that Rievaulx was Clairvaux' daughter house in England, and that Bernard felt personally responsible for the still young community. William, Abbot of Rievaulx, was one of Bernard's right-hand men, and the Rievaulx monks, for their part, felt honoured to think of Bernard as their immediate father. The fact that Bernard asked Aelred to write this work speaks volumes for the degree of sanctity that Aelred had already achieved while still novice master at Rievaulx. To have impressed Bernard to such a degree he must have been a truly remarkable monk, as outstanding in spiritual experience as he was in monastic observance.

* * *

In resuming here the chapters which we have omitted from our translation, we should like to repeat that we have only done so in order that the theme of the work may be easier to follow. These chapters are by no means lacking in interest. *Part I, chapter 6*, of the original work, fits in between chapters five and six of the present translation. It is a philosophical digression. In any consideration about God, Aelred says, there are bound to be those who claim that He does not exist. But only a fool could say in his heart that there is no God (*Psalm* xiii. 1). Aelred, taking up cudgels with the fool, asks him who is wise, in his estimation. Do you take no account of what wise men say? he asks. Even if not one single man were endowed with wisdom, wisdom would exist none the less, in its own right. If wisdom did not exist, there would be no possibility of men becoming wise. The fool might suggest that at least the angels are wise, even if he can find no wise man. But not even an angel, Aelred insists, can derive wisdom from its own being. When the fool asks where he may find the wisdom that will make him wise, his interlocutor senses that he has made his point. 'You must admit, then, that wisdom exists, to be found at the end of the search by those who seek to become wise. If it did not already exist, you could not possibly find it.' But the fool is not quite convinced yet. He prefers to hold that wisdom is not found by seeking. It comes, he says, 'by knowledge, and by the use of our minds'. But this, to Aelred, seems too much like putting on wisdom as one puts on clothes.

'You *must* obtain your wisdom from somewhere', he pleads, 'and if you say you got it from a wise man, he in turn must have got it from some other wise man. Even if we acquired wisdom from the angels, they would have had to get it from someone else first.' True wisdom enters holy souls so that they may become wise, but has this happened to the fool? He is probably not even conscious of his own existence. He might say that he never doubted his own existence, in which case Aelred would ask, 'Did you always exist then? Where did your being come from?' At least the fool admits that his being, at least, comes from another. When asked from where this other comes, the fool brings in his previous stand-by, the angel. But even an angel, repeats Aelred (one feels with some weariness), must have his being from someone else. 'Obviously we are forced to the conclusion that *all* things have their being from an uncreated being, and that *all* wisdom is derived from uncreated wisdom.'

*   *   *

Having thus proved God's existence, Aelred comes back to his original proposition. We go away from God through the misuse of love, which is concupiscence, and return to Him by using love in the way it was meant to be used, namely as charity. Still in the context of going away from God and returning to Him, we come, in

Part I, chapters 11 *to* 15, to the question of free will as a medium between concupiscence and charity. (This excursus may be read between chapter nine and ten of the translation.) Free will,

Aelred explains, means will, but in the special sense of choice and desire, and this will is something that goes together with reason. It is in free will that we find the point between true and false love, the choice between good and evil, between concupiscence and charity. The free will can choose between alternatives.

God must be, in some sense, the instigator of a good will, for without Him we can do nothing. Aelred takes the example of Saint Paul to prove his point. 'If I do this (preaching) willingly, I have a reward, but if against my will, a dispensation is committed to me' (1 *Corinthians* ix. 17). If it is no choice of Paul's, his preaching becomes merely a responsibility entrusted to him. If he does the work simply because he chooses to do so, he would be entitled to a reward. Therefore, in order that the deed done by God in us, and through us, may be our action as well as God's, it must attract the consent of the will. Then we shall be entitled to the reward that the deed deserves. If we will to perform a good action, however, it is because God brings about that we should will it. God stirs the will to seek and find.

Paul's example is a useful one for Aelred's purpose. He had once blasphemed Christ's name and persecuted the Church. His will had been perverted, and he had deserved the worst of punishments. But God gave Paul his mercy, so that he might be faithful and trustworthy . . . it is as if Paul were saying that no good was apparent in him at one time, but what good is there now is the work of God's mercy, which is given so that he may be trustworthy in fulfilling his mission. Paul readily admits, even when claiming that he has worked harder than some others in the Lord's service, that this is not due to himself. I have worked harder, he says, but adds 'It was not I. . . .' The work sprang not from Paul's powers, or Paul's wisdom, but from God's grace. Now this might seem as if Paul's free will is diminished in some way, but in fact the contrary is true. The grace of God was with him precisely to *bring about his consent* to work on the Lord's behalf. He was a willing collaborator with God. If God had worked in him without using Paul's will, Paul could not have said that he had fought the good fight and kept the faith. God brought all Paul's good works to perfection, inclining his will to perform the divine will by some secret inspiration. Consent made Paul's free will one with God's will. God worked through Paul, and brought it about that Paul's work came to completion. The concept of consent is all important here, since it describes of itself quite exactly how the human will and the divine will work together. It means agreement, feeling together, thinking together, an identification between two wills which remain none the less distinct.

Before concluding that grace does not take away our free will, and that free will does not diminish the effectiveness of grace, Aelred considers two further points. The first question is whether we shall have a will to consent to the goodness of our reward in heaven, and a reason that will judge that reward to be the most perfect possible good for us. The answer is the obvious one that we cannot choose evil in heaven. The second question concerns children who die before having used reason or will. Like animals, they cannot merit salvation or damnation, as far as Aelred can see. He claims that 'many such children are saved by the clear workings of grace, so that they both merit and receive salvation', but no explanation is given.

Aelred next considers (in his chapter 13) the claim of an objector who says that reason, without any stimulus to evil, is of its nature inclined to good. Aelred's reply to this is that every creature created out of nothing is necessarily subject to change. By some natural impulse resulting from its changeableness, it always has a tendency towards the nothingness of its origin. There is no principle of permanence or stability in nature. A creature always stands in need of grace, the grace of God by whose power it was created, in order to curb its impermanence, to raise it to higher things, and to keep it from tending to the lower things to which its instability inclines it.

Changeableness is natural to man and angel, for Aelred. This explains why grace is necessary always, even in heaven where no evil can dominate. He considers grace in two ways, firstly as creating (giving a good will) and then as helping (giving the ability to persevere where the will has consented). Whether or not the reprobate may be given these graces, to inspire them with a good will, and to give them perseverance, he will not say. 'At least', he says, 'I will say that the elect receive more grace than did Adam and Eve in paradise, because they have more to suffer. They have greater weaknesses to contend with, and therefore are given a greater power of resistance to evil. We know that Adam and Eve were given the power to persevere if they wanted to. They were given a good will. But the elect are enabled to persevere, and they do in fact persevere. This is something over and above their good will.

'When we consider the case of those who have no such good will, we can see that they cannot get it of their own powers, nor, if they had it, would they be able to maintain it with their own strength. . . . If it seems unjust that they should be blamed for having no good will (and no one can have it unless it comes as a free gift) at least they have reason, and their culpability consists of a misuse of judgement in choosing properly.' Thus God is not unjust in condemning the reprobate. Aelred's argument for the justice of God in condemning completely innocent children, 'whom creation did not make evil, nor their own will make unjust', is less satisfactory. 'Think of the whole human race', he suggests, 'as a dead tree, rotten to the root, poisoned by the devil, justly condemned to die. A few twigs are saved, and grafted on to the tree of life, Christ. If the dead tree should ask why am I abandoned, God answers: "Is your eye evil because I am good? (*St. Matthew* xx. 15). What I have given to many was in no way owed to them. Jacob I have loved but Esau I have hated" (*Romans* ix. 13).'

The answer is obviously not a very satisfactory one, and the mysterious problem comes nearest a solution, for Aelred, in a later chapter, also summarized in this appendix (p. 149). Aelred shows how conscious he is that he has offended God gravely, and that all sin is an offence against God. The sheer truth of this perception makes a severe conclusion reasonable. God is not in a position to be questioned, as far as man is concerned.

* * *

Chapters 26 *to* 30 of the original *Speculum* (to be read in the translation between chapters 19 and 20) are clearly a digression, since Aelred laments having to include the subject of sin at all. The digression forms a mole, he says, on an otherwise beautiful body. He will at least not go into details, for fear of offending Bernard, who is so pure and holy, but he feels he must say something about the pleasures in which men seek delight—pleasures of the eyes, and of the other senses, and also the lust for power. Solomon, in the days when he was less wise, said, 'I will go and abound with delights' (*Ecclesiastes* ii. 1), but when he turned to all the works which his hands had wrought, the houses, the vineyards, the trained singers, he saw 'in all things vanity and vexation of mind', and that 'nothing was lasting under the sun'. To these words Aelred adds those of Our Lord in St. John viii: 'He who does sin is the slave of sin.' There is, however, nothing servile about the Sabbath of which Aelred is speaking, for it allows of no servile works whatever.

'If the Son has freed you, you are freed', and with this freedom Aelred connects the invitation of St. Matthew xi. 28: *Come to me all you that labour and are burdened, and I will refresh you.* Refreshment is a preparation for the Sabbath. *Take My yoke upon you*, says our Sabbath, Christ, *and learn of me because I am meek and humble of heart, and you shall find rest to your souls* (*St. Matthew* xi. 29). The yoke is peace and Sabbath rest. Instead of burdening, it unites us to God. It has no weight, instead it gives us wings. The Holy Spirit, the sevenfold gift, comes on the seventh day of rest, and charity is diffused in our hearts by the same Holy Spirit who is given to us.

Then comes Aelred's confession of past misdeeds, which he surely does in imitation of his favourite Saint Augustine. His reason for making such a confession here is simply to repeat what a miracle of grace his conversion was. He knew good fortune in the world, in his youth, and above all he had prized friendship. But all things, including friendship, come to an end, in the world, and besides, 'the beginning (of friendship) was never completely innocent, while as it developed it was never blameless. Its end could not be without condemnation.' Thus fear grew in him, as he discovered how a life of self-indulgence must result in destruction. Yet all the time the envious spoke of him as someone who had everything, someone who was really well off, and to whom nothing was ever lacking.

Gradually, however, the love of Jesus grew within him, and he saw at last the possibility of a love that need never come to an end, never have any evil of wrong-doing, and yet be crowned with the highest reward. 'In Thy love there is no offence to be feared, the only possible offence being the wilful desertion of that love. There is no suspicion, for Christ can see right into the heart. There is peace, because anger is done away, and security, because the world is despised.' The flesh weighed heavily even after Aelred's conversion, but, as he says, the chains were broken at last, and Paradise was offered to him, as it is offered to repentant publicans and prostitutes. 'Now Beloved', he says to the Lord, 'I can breathe again, and rest under Thy burden, for Thy yoke is sweet, Thy burden light.'

It is sad, he reflects, that many people think of the Lord's burden as heavy. But if we find it heavy, we cannot blame the yoke, it is only our concupiscence that causes us pain. 'My strength was diminished in Babylon. I am free now, but still the worse off for having been captive there in time past. Until I am fully healed I shall always suffer this weakness, that is to say until such time as this corruptible body puts on incorruption.' He deals extensively in Part II with the fact that the weakness resulting from habits of sin is responsible for any suffering a monk finds in the religious life, and that it is not the yoke of Christ that irks him. 'Those who complain of the severity of the Lord's yoke', he writes in his chapter 30, 'are possibly weighed down by the yoke of worldly desires. They may be outwardly good religious, and inwardly covetous men. They bear unnecessary burdens manufactured by themselves. They fast, yet inwardly they are gluttons. Outwardly they dress in a penitential habit, but inwardly they are thirsting after worldly honour and glory. Dressed in priestly vestments, they may be stained by the filth of the flesh. Dressed in white wool, as innocent lambs (a reference to some Cistercians?), they are as avaricious as ravening wolves, adding house to house and field to field, sparing neither widows nor orphans. They spend the alms of poor men on themselves, and quarrel about benefactions, for which they are always ready to take up lawsuits. . . .' The yoke is none the less a light burden in itself, and Aelred confesses himself willing to bear any suffering, for he knows he has sinned against God, and against none other: *tibi soli peccavi*.

★   ★   ★

The first part of the *Speculum* ends with Aelred's lament for his friend Simon, which is incorporated into the work in a manner similar to that of Bernard's lament for Gerard in his sermons on the Song of Songs. The purpose also is similar. Simon, like Gerard, was a model religious and a very close friend. The love of God had found an ideal subject in them both. But there is a further relevance in what Aelred has to say about Simon, since his friend had abandoned the world in order to embrace the severest possible form of life. Saint Bernard wanted Aelred's *Speculum* to be a refutation of the errors of those who claimed that the monastic life need not necessarily be a very hard one. This is an incidental preoccupation throughout the present work, and Simon's example can be quoted as something of an ideal to be followed by others. His conversion to the monastic life had been all the more remarkable, Aelred tells us, because he had been 'a tender, delicate youth, noble and beautiful'. He had never been strong; indeed, he had known illness from an early age, and the last eight years of his life had brought such sufferings that he could find no pleasure in anything external at all. Yet he had always been cheerful, kind, affable, and invariably quiet and recollected. Aelred had taken Simon as his model, correcting himself by observing his friend.

'I used to embrace you in my heart', Aelred muses, 'and kiss you, not with my lips, but with my love. I loved you, and you took me as a friend from the time I entered the monastery.' And now Simon is with Jesus, at heaven's banquet. There is no real need to weep for him, none the less the sweet memory of a beloved brother does reduce him to tears. Losing Simon is like losing a father, a son, and a friend at the same time, so that Aelred's grief is threefold. His death had been all the more a shock for its suddenness. Simon had been ill, but seemed to be improving. All the brethren were sleeping at the time, and only one monk was watching by his side. Simon said '*Miseri-*

151

cordiam . . .' three times, as if he were trying to begin the hundredth psalm, *Misericordiam et judicium cantabo tibi Domine.* He turned to the monk at his side and repeated the word over and over again, as if delighting both in the sound and thought: 'Mercy and judgement I will sing to Thee, O Lord.' What does it mean? Aelred asks, and suggests that Simon could feel all his sins disappearing in a vast ocean of security, mercy and peace. 'Go then, into your rest', he bids his friend, 'into God's tabernacle. Open wide your bosom, Father Abraham, and may there be a place for me, at his side.'

*   *   *

Part III, chapter 35 of the original *Speculum* is a lengthened version of an essay written probably earlier in Aelred's monastic career. It takes the form of a disputation with an Augustinian canon on the aim and scope of the monastic profession. Again, it is easy to see why Aelred incorporated the disputation here, since he had been asked by Bernard to defend the monastic life against those who either sought, or unconsciously tended, to water down the austerities of the Cistercian rule. Aelred admits that 'this is something in the nature of a digression . . . but it is still to the point of our discussion. Since we are monks, we must carefully consider everything that has to do with our way of life. In our Rule there is much written about what we have to do with our bodies, as well as what we do with our souls. The whole purpose of our life is contained in the Rule. Now this Augustinian claims that the essence of the monastic life is not in the practices laid down in the Rule, but in a special something else which gives all the practices enjoined their worth and savour.

'But what is this something', Aelred asks, 'unless it be *everything* to which we have bound ourselves by our vows? The Augustinian considers that many points are not essential to the Rule because Saint Benedict allows them to be dispensed for the weaker brethren. Such points are manual work, the measure and quality of food, a certain type of bed, and the habit of staying inside the monastery. Aelred is amazed that the Augustinian can consider these things merely adjuncts, and not of the

152

essence of the Rule. What is the Rule, he asks, if it is not all these different things that Saint Benedict lays down for his monks? The only difference between one religious rule and another is in clothes, food, the time spent in psalmody and reading, the manner of performing the chapter of faults, and so on. These vary from one Rule to another, and the Rule, he argues, cannot be kept without the observance of all the precepts it contains.

This tends to make Aelred seem rather a stickler for rules and regulations, but he goes on to put his argument in a wider perspective which explains his stand. 'If anyone should ask if a monk is still a monk who follows all the observances and is yet proud, argumentative, and impatient, my answer is this. If a monk sins against the law of God and corrects these very faults by the means laid down in the Rule, he is observing the Rule. If, on the other hand, he considers the Rule as some kind of instrument by means of which he may eliminate his faults, and observe the Lord's precepts more easily, it may happen that he abuses this excellent instrument in some way, and so neither acquires virtues, nor loses his vices. He fulfils none of Christ's law and finds in the Rule his own condemnation.' Thus, for Aelred, there are two abuses equally to be guarded against. The first is in ignoring regulations because they do not seem to be essential to the Rule. The second is in observing them, yet making a mockery of them by not progressing in charity, which is always the fundamental aim.

NOTES

INTRODUCTION AND PART I

[1] *St. Bernard of Clairvaux* (Mowbray, 1960), p. 71.
[2] *Prudentius*, ed. H. J. Thompson, in Loeb Classical Library.
[3] *The Rule of St. Benedict*, conclusion of the prologue.
[4] *Christian Friendship*, by Aelred of Rievaulx, trans. C. H. Talbot, London, 1942.
[5] Psalm ciii. 2.
[6] Ibid. ciii. 21.
[7] Ibid. ciii. 15.
[8] Exodus v. 7.
[9] 1 St. John iv. 8.
[10] Genesis i. 31.
[11] Ecclesiasticus xxxix. 31.
[12] Psalm xlviii. 13.
[13] Ibid. lxxii. 28.
[14] Ibid. lxxii. 27.
[15] Ibid. xxxviii. 7.
[16] Colossians ii. 14–15.
[17] Deuteronomy xxxii. 10.
[18] Psalm liv. 7.
[19] Ibid. xxi. 28.
[20] Ibid. xiii. 1.
[21] Here Aelred gives his arguments for the existence of God. See appendix, p. 144.
[22] Psalm cxxxviii. 6.
[23] St. Matthew xxi. 7.
[24] Canticle i. 3.
[25] Ibid. viii. 14.
[26] St. Luke xv. 21.
[27] Ephesians iv. 23.
[28] St. John xiii. 34.
[29] Acts xvii. 28.
[30] From the *Phenomena* of Aratus.
[31] Romans vii. 16.
[32] Galatians v. 17.
[33] 1 St. John ii. 16.
[34] Aelred's treatment of the questions of grace and free will (Chapters XI to XV in the original) is summarized in the appendix, p. 145.
[35] St. Matthew xxii. 40.
[36] 1 Corinthians xiii. 4–6.
[37] Psalm xxx. 20.
[38] Song of Songs i. 3.
[39] Habacuc iii. 18.
[40] Genesis ii. 3.
[41] Ibid. i. 5.
[42] Ibid. i. 8.

[43] Psalm xxxii. 9.
[44] St. John v. 20.
[45] Ibid. xv. 10.
[46] St. Matthew iii. 17.
[47] Zacharias iii. 9.
[48] Apocalypse iv. 5.
[49] St. Luke vi. 20; St. Matthew v. 5; St. Luke vi. 21.
[50] Ecclesiastes v. 12.
[51] Song of Songs v. 2.
[52] Psalm iv. 9.
[53] Ecclesiastes v. 9.
[54] Habacuc ii. 6.
[55] 1 Timothy vi. 17.
[56] St. Matthew xxv. 35.
[57] 1 Timothy vi. 9.
[58] St. Matthew vi. 31 and 33.
[59] Hebrews x. 34.
[60] Wisdom v. 3, 7–10, 13–15.
[61] *Vide infra* Part III, ch. 35.
[62] The unpleasant 'mole' which Aelred felt obliged to impose here on the body of his *Speculum* is summarized in the appendix, p. 148. In the original the subject covers Chapters XXVI to XXX.
[63] Isaias xl. 6–7.
[64] St. Matthew v. 45.
[65] Ibid. xi. 30.
[66] 1 Corinthians xiii. 4.
[67] Psalm lxxiii. 19.
[68] Genesis viii. 4.
[69] Leviticus xxvi. 6.
[70] Isaias lxvi. 23.
[71] Deuteronomy vi. 5.
[72] Romans xiii. 7.
[73] Ibid.
[74] See appendix, p. 151, for a résumé of Aelred's chapter on the death of his friend Simon which brings Part I to a close.

PART II

[1] St. Matthew xi. 29.
[2] 1 St. John ii. 16.
[3] 1 Timothy vi. 10.
[4] 1 St. John ii. 16.
[5] St. James iv. 1.
[6] The work of Hippocrates on 'Air, Waters and Places' is extensively quoted in Galen's thesis 'that the mental faculties follow the physical constitution'. This is probably the sort of theory that Aelred has in mind. It makes psychology a department of physiology, so that the claims of the body are emphasized in any question of the psyche. This seems reasonable to us to-day with our psycho-somatic approach to many medical problems; but Aelred, as a typical disciple of Bernard, had no time for it. He would claim that consolation abounds precisely where suffering most abounds.
[7] 2 Corinthians vii. 5.

[8] Philippians iii. 8.
[9] Ibid. i. 23.
[10] Galatians vi. 14.
[11] 1 Corinthians xvi. 22.
[12] 2 Corinthians i. 3–4.
[13] Ibid. i. 5.
[14] St. Benedict, *Regula Monachorum*, prologue.
[15] Proverbs xxxi. 6.
[16] Psalm xciii. 19.
[17] 1 Corinthians xii. 31.
[18] St. Matthew vii. 23.
[19] Numbers xxiii. 10.
[20] Ibid. xi.
[21] Judges ii. 5.
[22] St. Matthew xxvii. 4.
[23] Ecclesiasticus xxxiv. 30.
[24] Romans viii. 28.
[25] Psalm lxxvi. 3.
[26] Ibid. xxv. 2 and Ibid. cxxxviii. 23.
[27] Ibid. cxxxi. 14.
[28] Proverbs i. 7.
[29] St. John vi. 61.
[30] St. Luke xiv. 10.
[31] Ibid. xxi. 34.
[32] St. Matthew v. 22.
[33] Ibid. xx. 27.
[34] Ibid. vii. 12.
[35] Ibid. xii. 36.
[36] Romans xiii. 14.
[37] 2 Timothy ii. 4.
[38] 1 Thessalonians iv. 10–11.
[39] 2 Thessalonians iii. 10.
[40] St. James ii. 1.
[41] Ibid. iii. 16.
[42] Ibid. iv. 4.
[43] 1 St. Peter ii. 11.
[44] Ibid. ii. 1.
[45] Ibid. iv. 11.
[46] Ibid. v. 2.
[47] Ibid. v. 5.
[48] Ibid. v. 8.
[49] 1 St. John ii. 4.
[50] Ibid. iii. 15.
[51] St. Jude 16.
[52] Ibid. 23.
[53] St. John xiv. 23.
[54] Malachias iii. 14.
[55] Psalm lxxii. 13.
[56] Acts xiv. 21.
[57] 1 Thessalonians iii. 3.
[58] Exodus xv. 22–27.
[59] St. Matthew vii. 13.

[60] St. Luke xxii. 28.
[61] Exodus xvi. 20.
[62] St. Matthew xi. 30.
[63] Job x. 15.
[64] Colossians iii. 5.
[65] Ibid. lxxii. 23.
[66] Apocalypse iii. 17.
[67] Psalm vi. 3.
[68] 1 Corinthians vi. 17.
[69] St. Gregory,
[70] St. John xiv. 21.
[71] Virgil, Eclogues II, 65: *Trahit sua quemquam voluptas.*
[72] Ecclesiasticus ii. 1.
[73] 2 Corinthians i. 3–5.
[74] Psalm xxx. 20.
[75] Romans xi. 8.
[76] St. Matthew xxv. 41.
[77] Philippians iv. 11–12.
[78] St. Augustine, *Confessions*, X, 33.
[79] 2 Corinthians iv. 18.
[80] Psalm xliv. 14.
[81] Galatians vi. 4.
[82] Job xxxii. 19.
[83] Deuteronomy vi. 16.
[84] 1 Corinthians x. 9.

PART III

[1] Leviticus xxiii and xxv.
[2] St. Matthew xxii. 37–40.
[3] Ephesians v. 29.
[4] 1 St. John iv. 20.
[5] St. Matthew xxii. 37.
[6] Romans xiii. 9.
[7] Psalm cxxxii. 1.
[8] St. Luke xiv. 26.
[9] Exodus xx. 12.
[10] St. Matthew v. 43.
[11] Ibid. v. 46.
[12] Ibid. v. 44.
[13] St. Matthew vi. 12.
[14] St. John viii. 34.
[15] Ibid. i. 14.
[16] St. Luke ii. 25.
[17] Ibid. vii. 34 *et seq.*
[18] St. John viii. 4. The woman taken in adultery, traditionally identified with Magdalen (St. John xx. 17).
[19] Psalm xliv. 3.
[20] Isaias liii. 7.
[21] St. Luke xxiii. 34.
[22] 1 Corinthians ii. 8.
[23] Leviticus xxv. 10.

[24] St. John vii. 39.
[25] Romans v. 25.
[26] To put this logical classification very simply, Aelred is saying that charity is a sub-division of love, or a particular kind of love.
[27] St. Matthew iv. 10.
[28] Deuteronomy vi. 5; St. Mark xii. 30.
[29] Philemon i. 20.
[30] Part II, ch. 7 to 12.
[31] 2 Kings xiii.
[32] 2 Corinthians xi. 25.
[33] Philippians iv. 13.
[34] 1 Kings xviii.
[35] Exodus ii. 16.
[36] 2 Kings xvii. 27.
[37] 3 Kings ii. 7.
[38] Ephesians v. 29.
[39] Isaias xlix. 15.
[40] 1 Timothy v. 8.
[41] Genesis xlvii. 29.
[42] 3 Kings xlii. 24.
[43] Genesis xlii. 24.
[44] 2 Kings xviii. 5.
[45] St. Matthew xxiii. 37.
[46] Ibid. xxiii. 38.
[47] Romans ix. 3.
[48] Hebrews xi. 23.
[49] 2 Kings xi. 2.
[50] 3 Kings xi. 4.
[51] Ecclesiastes vii. 17.
[52] Acts xiii. 2.
[53] 2 Timothy i. 4.
[54] St. Luke xiv. 26.
[55] 1 Timothy v. 8.
[56] Ephesians v. 29.
[57] 2 Timothy iii. 2.
[58] Ibid.
[59] Saint Augustine: Tractatus 51 *In Joannem.*
[60] 1 St. John ii. 16.
[61] Joel iii. 3.
[62] 1 Kings xxiii. 17.
[63] Genesis xxxvii.
[64] Numbers xii. 3.
[65] 3 Kings ii. 23.
[66] 1 Kings xx. 41.
[67] 2 Kings xviii. 33.
[68] St. Matthew xxvi. 39.
[69] Titus ii. 12.
[70] Ibid. i. 15.
[71] 1 Timothy iv. 3.
[72] St. Luke xxi. 34.
[73] 1 Thessalonians iv. 4.
[74] 1 Timothy ii. 9.

[75] 1 Corinthians xi. 20.
[76] Ibid. xi. 21–22.
[77] 1 Corinthians x. 20.
[78] Ibid. x. 28.
[79] Tobias ii. 21.
[80] St. Luke iii. 8.
[81] Psalm liii. 8.
[82] St. Matthew xix. 21.
[83] Ibid. xix. 12.
[84] The disputation with an Augustinian Canon which Aelred inserts at this point, is summarized in the appendix, p. 152.
[85] Saint Benedict's Rule, Chapter 41.
[86] Ibid. Chapter 48.
[87] Ibid. Chapter 48.
[88] St. Matthew xxii. 39.
[89] Romans ix. 3.
[90] Ephesians v. 29.
[91] St. Matthew xxii. 39.
[92] 1 St. John iii. 16.
[93] Philippians ii. 4.
[94] 1 Corinthians ix. 22.
[95] Genesis vii.
[96] Philemon i. 20.
[97] St. John xix. 26.
[98] 1 Corinthians i. 30.
[99] 1 Timothy i. 5.
[100] Proverbs xxvii. 6.